C000017535

MUSIC ★ ICONS

# HENDRIX

LUKE CRAMPTON & DAFYDD REES
WITH WELLESLEY MARSH

**TASCHEN**

HONG KONG  KÖLN  LONDON  LOS ANGELES  MADRID  PARIS  TOKYO

# CONTENTS

# JIMI HENDRIX: EXPERIENCE

Arguably the most influential rock guitarist of all time, the life and career of Jimi Hendrix shone like a crazy diamond—and perhaps more than any other legendary artist—truly burned out before it faded away at just 27 years of age. Although (bizarrely) Janis Joplin, Brian Jones, Jim Morrison and Kurt Cobain also burnt out at two-score-and-seven, no other musician who died in his twenties has left such an indelible mark on the history of popular music.

On November 27, 1942 in Seattle, Johnny Allen Hendrix was born to his 22-year old military-serving father, James 'Al' Hendrix, and 17-year old mother, Lucille Jeter. With his name changed at the age of four to James Marshall Hendrix, he grew up in a poor, dysfunctional environment, his parents divorcing when he was nine and time spent living with his grandmother in Vancouver. A quiet and sensitive child, his world was opened up by music, listening intently to his father's blues records by the likes of B.B. King, Elmore James and Muddy Waters. Having played on a one-string ukulele as a kid, Hendrix bought a used acoustic guitar for $5 at the age of 14, before being given an electric Supro Ozark at 17 by his father. A natural southpaw, he was a quick and devoted learner, unusually honing his craft to play the right-handed instruments with his left hand; he also began mimicking the stage antics of the freshman class of rock 'n' roll, notably Little Richard, Chuck Berry and Elvis Presley (whom he saw live in 1957) as a member of the local Seattle combo, the Rocking Kings.

Dropping out of school in his senior year and flirting with petty crime, Hendrix enlisted in the army serving for one year as a supply clerk with the 101st Airborne Paratroopers Division. While there he teamed up with fellow soldier, Billy Cox, fronting the King Kasuals which relocated to Nashville to play in the burgeoning local R&B scene.

Critical to his subsequent success and growing guitar chops, Hendrix then served a substantial and varied apprenticeship as a lead and rhythm guitarist for dozens of traveling artists. Moving to Harlem in 1964, he secured more live work as guitarist for the Isley Brothers and his erstwhile hero, Little Richard. Increasingly in demand for session work, Hendrix signed an ill-advised recording contract in 1965 with Ed Chalpin.

By now an accomplished guitarist and showman, Hendrix formed his own group, Jimmy James & the Blue Flames in 1966, which played a sturdy mix of R&B, blues standards and original material at popular residencies around New York's Greenwich Village. That year Animals' bassist (and would-be manager) Chas Chandler saw him perform and, duly impressed, suggested Hendrix relocate to London.

Word of Hendrix's dazzling talent quickly spread in the United Kingdom, and admiration from the likes of Eric Clapton, Brian Jones, Pete Townshend and Jeff Beck confirmed that Hendrix was a powerful and innovative new force in the burgeoning hard-rock/blues scene. His subsequent meteoric rise to become a global star lasted only four years however. Increasingly beset by legal problems, the breakup of his band, a relentless schedule, the hysteria and adulation which had catapulted him to worldwide celebrity and a drug bust in Toronto, it was narcotics (prescription and nonprescription) and alcohol which ultimately provided his only place of solace—and, conversely, caused his premature demise.

Hendrix became the poster boy for the psychedelic era's sex, drugs and rock 'n' roll lifestyle. His flamboyant hippie style and colorful dress only added to his groundbreaking showmanship. His musical prowess was conversely powerful and heavy and at times, sensual and soft. A profound songwriter and distinctive vocalist, it was his extraordinary guitar-playing which revolutionized music. He radiated talent and imagination making bold sonic experiments with wah-wah, feedback manipulation, fuzzy distortions, foot-pedal effects, guitar immolation, stacks of beefed-up amplifiers and mind-bending fret work which revealed truly liquid riffs. Sometimes playing his favored Fender Stratocaster behind his back or with his teeth, Hendrix single-handedly built the bridge between blues rock and hard rock and laid the foundations for what would become heavy metal.

He left an unrivaled canon of experimental guitar genius, and a brace of timeless classics. In addition, more than 300 unreleased recordings, a perennially top-selling back catalog—and a legal minefield which resulted in years of unpleasant litigation. Hendrix's powerful impact and legacy resulted in his posthumous induction into the Rock and Roll Hall of Fame, the UK Music Hall of Fame, and a star on the Hollywood Walk of Fame. The inspiration behind the Experience Music Project and museum in Seattle, his **Are You Experienced** album was subsequently inducted into the United States National Recording Registry, while **Rolling Stone** placed Hendrix at No. 1 on its 100 Greatest Guitarists of All Time list in 2003.

Transforming the landscape of rock music forever, Jimi Hendrix broke bold new ground and his dexterous guitar skills continue to influence successive generations of musicians. His music, style and legend burn as brightly today as they did 40 years ago. Kiss the sky.

# JIMI HENDRIX: EXPERIENCE

Jimi Hendrix war vermutlich der einflussreichste Rockgitarrist aller Zeiten, seine Karriere funkelte wie ein Diamant, ein Feuerwerk, das erst sprühte und dann ausbrannte, noch bevor sein Leben zu Ende ging, als er erst 27 Jahre alt war. Seltsamerweise starben auch Janis Joplin, Brian Jones, Jim Morrison und Kurt Cobain im gleichen Alter, doch kein anderer so früh verstorbene Musiker hat so unauslöschliche Spuren in der Geschichte der Popmusik hinterlassen.

Johnny Allen Hendrix kam am 2. November 1942 in Seattle als Sohn des 22-jährigen amerikanischen Soldaten James ‚Al' Hendrix und der 17-jährigen Lucille Jeter zur Welt. Als er vier Jahre alt war, benannten seine Eltern ihren Sohn, der in ärmlichen Verhältnissen aufwuchs, in James Marshall Hendrix um. Seine Eltern ließen sich scheiden, als er neun Jahre alt war; er lebte längere Zeit bei seiner Großmutter in Vancouver. Dem stillen und sensiblen Kind öffnete sich erst durch die Musik eine neue Welt; gebannt hörte er zu, wenn die Blues-Schallplatten seines Vaters liefen: B.B. King, Elmore James und Muddy Waters. Als Kind spielte er auf einer einsaitigen Ukulele und kaufte sich mit 14 seine erste gebrauchte Gitarre für fünf Dollar. Als er 17 war, bekam er von seinem Vater die erste E-Gitarre, eine Supro Ozark. Jimi Hendrix war zwar Linkshänder, lernte aber schnell und arbeitete hartnäckig und ausdauernd daran, das Spiel mit der linken Hand auf den rechtshändigen Instrumenten zu verbessern. Er fing auch an, mit seiner Band, den Rocking Kings, im heimischen Seattle die Bühnenshow der Gründerväter des Rock 'n' Roll nachzuahmen und imitierte vor allem Little Richard, Chuck Berry und Elvis Presley (den er 1957 live auf der Bühne erlebte).

Kurz vor dem Abschluss brach Jimi Hendrix in der 12. Klasse die Schule ab und hatte mit Kleinkriminalität zu tun, bevor er zur Armee ging und ein Jahr lang in der 101. Fallschirmjägereinheit diente. Dort freundete er sich mit seinem Kameraden Billy Cox an, mit dem er die Band The King Kasuals gründete, die 1962 nach Nashville weiterzog, um an der dort blühenden R&B-Szene teilzuhaben.

Entscheidend für Jimi Hendrixs späteren Erfolg und seine ständig perfekter werdende Gitarrentechnik war die ausgedehnte Lehrzeit als Lead- und Rhythmusgitarrist bei Dutzenden von Musikern. 1964 zog er nach Harlem, wo er als Gitarrist für die Isley Brothers und sein früheres großes Vorbild Little Richard Arbeit bei Live-Auftritten fand. Jimi Hendrix wurde immer öfter als Studiomusiker angefragt und unterschrieb 1965 einen Plattenvertrag mit Ed Chalpin, der sich später als sehr nachteilig für ihn erweisen sollte.

Jimi Hendrix war mittlerweile ein hervorragender Gitarrist und Showman geworden und gründete 1966 eine eigene Band, Jimmy James & the Blue Flames, die im New Yorker

Greenwich Village einen Mix aus R&B- und Blues-Standards und Eigenkompositionen spielte, der sehr gut ankam. In diesem Jahr erlebte ihn der Bassist (und spätere Manager) der Animals, Chas Chandler, bei einer Bühnenshow. Chandler war beeindruckt und schlug ihm vor, er solle doch nach London kommen.

Hendrixs Ruf als überragendes Talent breitete sich in England rasch aus. Die Bewunderung, die ihm von Eric Clapton, Brian Jones, Pete Townshend und Jeff Beck entgegengebracht wurde, bestätigte, dass Jimi Hendrix eine hervorragende und innovative neue Größe in der damals entstehenden Hardrock- und Blues-Szene war. Sein kometenhafter Aufstieg zum weltweiten Superstar sollte jedoch nur vier Jahre währen. Rechtsstreitigkeiten, das Zerbrechen seiner Band, ein gnadenlos ausgebuchter Tourkalender, der geradezu hysterische Personenkult, der mit einem unglaublich schnell einsetzenden Ruhm einherging, und eine Drogenrazzia in Toronto brachten Jimi Hendrix zunehmend in Bedrängnis. Legale und illegale Drogen und Alkohol waren das Einzige, was Jimi Hendrix Trost und Ruhe spendete – und seinen viel zu frühen Tod verursachte.

Hendrix wurde zur Ikone der psychedelischen Ära mit ihrem Lebensstil aus Sex, Drugs und Rock 'n' Roll. Sein extravagantes Auftreten und knallbunte Hippie-Kleidung machten seine einmalige Bühnenpräsenz noch aufsehenerregender. Sein musikalisches Können war von großer Kraft und Wuchtigkeit, dann wieder von Weichheit und Sinnlichkeit geprägt. Jimi Hendrix schrieb Stücke von großer Tiefe und sein Gesang war unnachahmlich, doch es war sein herausragendes Gitarrenspiel, mit dem er der Musikwelt völlig neue Impulse versetzte. Er sprühte nur so vor schöpferischer Kraft und Experimentierfreude und hatte keinerlei Berührungsängste bei Klangexperimenten mit Wah-Wah, Feedback, Verzerrung mit der Fuzzbox, Fußpedal-Klangeffekten, Gitarren-Opferritualen, aufeinandergestapelten Verstärkern und halsbrecherischer Fingerfertigkeit, durch die wahrhaft fließende Riffs zustande kamen. Manchmal spielte er seine Fender Stratocaster hinter dem Rücken oder mit den Zähnen. Es war Jimi Hendrix, der im Alleingang die Verbindung zwischen Bluesrock und Hardrock herstellte und das Fundament für den später entstehenden Heavy Metal legte.

Er hinterließ der Welt einen beispiellosen Kanon genial-experimenteller Gitarrensoli und eine Menge zeitloser Klassiker. Obendrein hinterließ Jimi Hendrix über 300 unveröffentlichte Aufnahmen, eine große Anzahl von Einspielungen mit ausgezeichneten, konstant bleibenden Verkaufszahlen – und ein juristisches Schlachtfeld, das zu jahrelangen Rechtsstreitigkeiten und Familienfehden über sein Erbe und seinen Nachlass führte. Jimi Hendrixs enorme Wirkung auch über seinen Tod hinaus führte dazu, dass er posthum in die Rock and Roll Hall of Fame und die britische Music Hall of Fame aufgenommen wurde und einen Stern auf dem Hollywood Walk of Fame bekam. Sein Album **Are You Experienced** diente dem Experience Music Project und Museum in Seattle als Inspiration und wurde in die United States National Recording Registry aufgenommen. Die Zeitschrift **Rolling Stone** ernannte Jimi Hendrix 2003 zur Nummer eins auf ihrer Liste der 100 größten Gitarristen aller Zeiten.

Jimi Hendrix hat die Rockmusik für immer verändert und unerschrocken neues Terrain für sie erobert. Mit seiner enormen Fingerfertigkeit und atemberaubenden Gitarrentechnik beeinflusst er bis heute Generationen von Musikern. Unvergessen sind seine Musik und sein Stil, sein Stern funkelt heute noch so hell wie vor vierzig Jahren. Kiss the sky.

# JIMI HENDRIX : L'EXPERIENCE

Jimi Hendrix est probablement le guitariste de rock le plus novateur et le plus adulé de tous les temps. Et à force de briller comme le « diamant fou » chanté par Pink Floyd – d'un éclat plus éblouissant que tout autre musicien de légende –, il s'est consumé tout entier jusqu'à s'éteindre, à seulement 27 ans. Alors que, fait étrange souvent souligné, Janis Joplin, Brian Jones, Jim Morrison et Kurt Cobain se sont aussi brûlé les ailes à l'âge de vingt-sept ans, aucun autre musicien mort trop jeune n'a laissé une empreinte aussi indélébile sur l'histoire de la musique populaire.

Johnny Allen Hendrix naît le 27 novembre 1942 à Seattle ; son père, James « Al » Hendrix, est un soldat de 22 ans, sa mère, Lucille Jeter, n'a que 17 ans. Sous le nouveau nom choisi par son père, James Marshall Hendrix grandit dans un environnement perturbé, frappé par la misère ; certains de ses frères et sœurs sont placés, ses parents divorcent quand il a neuf ans et il passe une partie de son adolescence chez sa grand-mère, à Vancouver. Enfant tranquille et sensible, il s'ouvre au monde grâce à la musique, en écoutant en boucle les disques de blues de son père : B.B. King, Elmore James ou Muddy Waters. Après avoir joué, enfant, sur un ukulélé à une seule corde, Hendrix se paie à l'âge de 14 ans une guitare acoustique d'occasion à 5 dollars ; l'année de ses 17 ans, son père lui offre une Supro Ozark électrique. Gaucher naturel, il apprend vite et avec passion, et en vient à suffisamment maîtriser son art pour jouer de la main gauche sur des instruments de droitiers. Au sein du groupe de jeunes local, les Rocking Kings, il commence à imiter la gestuelle des grands noms de la nouvelle scène rock 'n' roll, en particulier Little Richard, Chuck Berry et Elvis Presley (qu'il voit en concert en 1957).

Hendrix quitte le lycée en dernière année et commet de petits délits qui le poussent, pour éviter la prison, à s'engager dans l'armée en 1961. Il intègre pour un an la 101e division aéroportée avant d'être réformé et rencontre le soldat Billy Cox, avec lequel il forme les King Kasuals. Les deux amis s'installent à Nashville et écument la scène R&B locale.

Phase décisive pour la suite de sa carrière et sa maîtrise instrumentale, Hendrix fait son apprentissage en jouant avec des dizaines d'artistes. En 1964, il emménage à Harlem et trouve facilement des engagements comme guitariste de concert et de studio pour les Isley Brothers et son héros de toujours, Little Richard. De plus en plus sollicité, Hendrix signe un contrat d'exclusivité bien peu judicieux avec Ed Chalpin en 1965.

En 1966, devenu un guitariste et un homme de scène accompli, Hendrix forme son propre groupe, Jimmy James & the Blue Flames, qui joue un mélange puissant de R&B, de standards du blues et de compositions originales dans les lieux les plus branchés de Greenwich Village. Cette année-là, le bassiste des Animals Chas Chandler (qui deviendra son manager) le voit en concert et, très impressionné, lui conseille de s'installer à Londres.

La rumeur sur son talent éblouissant se répand vite au Royaume-Uni et l'admiration que lui vouent ses pairs Eric Clapton, Brian Jones, Pete Townshend ou Jeff Beck vient confirmer qu'Hendrix est une figure puissante et révolutionnaire de la nouvelle scène blues-rock. Ce livre montre son ascension fulgurante vers la célébrité et les étapes d'une carrière mondiale qui ne dura que quatre ans. Miné par les problèmes judiciaires, l'éclatement de son groupe, un agenda surchargé, son arrestation à Toronto pour détention de drogue et l'adulation hystérique de la foule qui l'a propulsé au sommet, Hendrix ne trouve plus de réconfort que dans les narcotiques (prescrits ou illicites) et l'alcool... qui provoqueront sa disparition prématurée.

Hendrix a incarné le style de vie « sex, drugs & rock 'n' roll » de l'ère psychédélique. Son style hippie et sa garde-robe flamboyante ne faisaient qu'ajouter à sa présence scénique inouïe. Ses prouesses musicales savaient s'exprimer avec une puissance pesante comme avec sensualité et douceur. Hendrix était un parolier inspiré et un chanteur unique, mais c'est son extraordinaire jeu de guitare qui a révolutionné la musique. Il irradiait le talent et l'imagination, se lançait dans des expérimentations sonores audacieuses en maniant comme personne avant lui wah-wah, larsen, distorsions, fuzz, effets de pédale, immolation de guitare, batteries d'amplificateurs saturés et gémissements sauvages, pour créer des riffs d'une fluidité totale. N'hésitant pas à jouer de sa Fender Stratocaster fétiche derrière son dos ou avec les dents, Hendrix a bâti à lui seul la passerelle entre le blues-rock et le hard-rock et posé les fondations de ce qui deviendra le heavy metal.

Il a laissé derrière lui une œuvre d'un génie expérimental sans égal, quelques classiques inusables, mais aussi un catalogue précieux, forcément lucratif, de plus de 300 enregistrements inédits – et un champ de mines juridique à l'origine de plusieurs années de litiges pitoyables. L'impact de Hendrix sur la musique lui vaut d'entrer, à titre posthume, au Rock and Roll Hall of Fame et au Music Hall of Fame britannique, et de recevoir son étoile sur le Hollywood Walk of Fame. À l'origine du projet « Experience Music » et du musée de Seattle, son album **Are You Experienced** est conservé au National Recording Registry américain et le magazine **Rolling Stone** a sacré Hendrix meilleur guitariste de tous les temps en 2003.

En transformant le paysage du rock de façon irréversible, Jimi Hendrix a pavé la voie à des générations de musiciens, électrisés et influencés par sa dextérité extatique à la guitare. Sa musique, son allure et sa légende flamboient avec autant d'ardeur aujourd'hui qu'il y a quarante ans. « Kiss the sky » – qu'il embrasse le ciel !

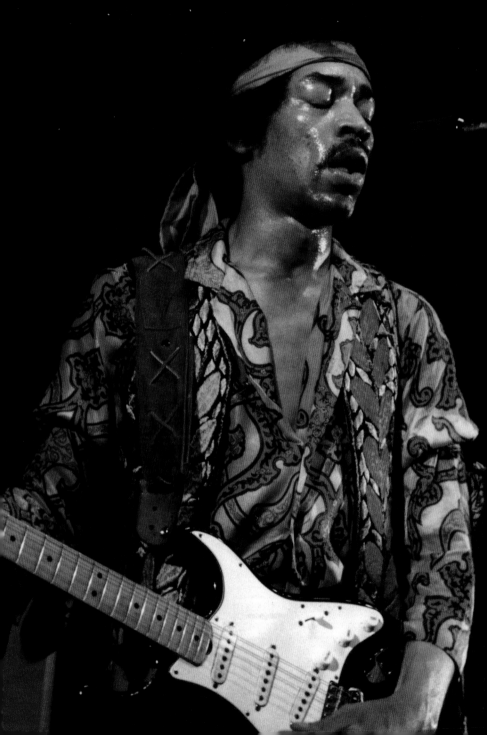

# 2
# CHRONOLOGY

CHRONOLOGIE

CHRONOLOGIE

# THE EARLY 1960$^S$

## DIE FRÜHEN 1960ER

## DÉBUT DES ANNÉES 1960

## 1958

Growing up in various poor accommodations in the multicultural area of Seattle's Central District, Jimi Hendrix was one of five siblings raised in an unstable and impoverished family by his father Al and aunt, Dolores. Currently attending Garfield High School, Jimi found solace in music, learning to play first an acoustic, then an electric guitar with natural fluency. Following his first gig at Seattle's Temple De Hirsch Sinai synagogue, Hendrix joins his first band, the Velvetones alongside saxophonist Luther Rabb, pianist Robert Green and others, playing regular Friday night rec room parties at the Yesler Terrace Neighborhood House housing project.

Jimi Hendrix und seine vier Geschwister wachsen in unsicheren und verarmten Verhältnissen bei seinem Vater Al und seiner Tante Dolores in der heruntergekommenen, multikulturellen Innenstadt Seattles, dem Central District, auf. Jimi besucht jetzt die Garfield High School, wo er einen Halt in der Musik findet und lernt, erst akustische und dann elektrische Gitarre zu spielen. Er hat seinen ersten Auftritt in der Synagoge von Seattle, dem Temple De Hirsch Sinai, und schließt sich zum ersten Mal einer Band an, den Velvetones mit Saxofonist Luther Rabb, Pianist Robert Green und anderen, die jeden Freitagabend im Partykeller der Sozialwohnungssiedlung Yesler Terrace Neighborhood House auftreten.

Jimi et ses quatre frères et sœurs grandissent dans un quartier multiculturel défavorisé du centre de Seattle auprès de leur père Al et de leur tante Dolores. Lycéen à la Garfield High School, Jimi trouve le réconfort dans la musique et démontre une aptitude naturelle à jouer de la guitare – d'abord acoustique, puis électrique. Après son premier concert à la synagogue Temple De Hirsch Sinai, à Seattle, Hendrix entre pour la première fois dans un groupe, les Velvetones (avec, entre autres, le saxophoniste Luther Rabb et le pianiste Robert Green); le groupe se produit tous les vendredis soirs dans la cave aménagée de la cité Yesler Terrace Neighborhood House.

## WEDNESDAY, MAY 31, 1961

After making his first paying performances as a member of R&B combo, the Rocking Kings, at Seattle's Washington Hall last year, Hendrix enlists in the army for three years at Fort Ord, California. He is posted to the 101st Airborne Paratroopers stationed at Fort Campbell, Kentucky, as a member of the elite Screaming Eagles squad, attaining the rank of Private First Class during his service. In November he will form the King Kasuals with fellow soldier and bassist, Billy Cox, initially playing at the Pink Poodle Club in Clarksville, Tennessee, which will subsequently become the house band at Club del Morocco in Nashville.

Nach den ersten bezahlten Konzerten mit der R&B-Combo The Rocking Kings in der Washington Hall in Seattle im Vorjahr tritt Hendrix seinen dreijährigen Wehrdienst in Fort Ord, Kalifornien, an. Er wird der in Fort Campbell, Kentucky, stationierten 101. Luftlande-Fallschirmjägereinheit zugeteilt. Er gehört der Elite-truppe der Screaming Eagles an und wird bis zum Obergefreiten befördert. Hendrix gründet zusammen mit einem Kameraden in Fort Campbell, dem Bassis-ten Billy Cox, die King Kasuals. Sie spielen anfangs im Pink Poodle Club in Clarksville, Tennessee, und wer-den später die Hausband im Club del Morocco in Nashville.

Après avoir gagné ses premiers cachets sur la scène du Washington Hall de Seattle l'année précédente avec les Rocking Kings, un groupe de R&B, Hendrix s'enrôle dans l'armée pour trois ans à Fort Ord (Cali-fornie). Il est affecté à la 101e division aéroportée sta-tionnée à Fort Campbell (Kentucky), où il rejoint le peloton d'élite des Screaming Eagles au sein duquel il atteint le grade de soldat de première classe. En novembre, Hendrix forme les King Kasuals avec son camarade de l'armée, le bassiste Billy Cox, à Fort Campbell ; ils font leurs débuts au Pink Poodle Club de Clarksville, dans le Tennessee, avant de devenir le groupe attitré du Club del Morocco de Nashville.

**MONDAY, JULY 2, 1962**

Hendrix is honorably discharged due to "medical unsuitability." Going on to team up with former band members in Bob Fisher & the Barnevilles, they tour the United States, backing the Marvelettes and Curtis Mayfield & the Impressions, before Hendrix moves to Vancouver, Canada, where he becomes a member of Bobbie Taylor & the Vancouvers, playing regularly at Dante's Inferno club.

Jimi Hendrix wird als „medizinisch untauglich" ehrenhaft aus der Armee entlassen. Er schließt sich seinen früheren Bandmitgliedern Bob Fisher & the Barnevilles an, mit denen er durch die USA tourt. Er spielt außerdem bei den Marvelettes und Curtis Mayfield & the Impressions, dann zieht er nach Vancouver, wo er Mitglied der Band Bobbie Taylor & the Vancouvers wird, die regelmäßig im Club Dante's Inferno auftritt.

Hendrix est réformé pour des raisons médicales. Il retrouve les membres de son ancien groupe et forme Bob Fisher & the Barnevilles, qui part en tournée américaine avec les Marvelettes et Curtis Mayfield & the Impressions. Hendrix part ensuite s'installer à Vancouver, au Canada, où il rejoint le groupe Bobbie Taylor & the Vancouvers, qui se produit régulièrement au club Dante's Inferno.

*"I was discharged from the services a month after Jimi and I began playing a Mickey Mouse bass. I was hard up and wondering where my next meal was coming from when Jimi phoned from New York and invited me to join him."*

*„Ich wurde einen Monat nach Jimi aus dem Wehrdienst entlassen und fing an, Mickymaus-Bass zu spielen. Ich hatte kein Einkommen und nichts zu beißen, da rief Jimi mich aus New York an, ob ich bei ihm mitspielen wolle."*

*« J'ai été réformé de l'armée un mois après Jimi et j'ai commencé à jouer de la basse. J'étais dans la galère à cette époque, tout le temps en train de me demander comment je paierais mon prochain repas, quand Jimi m'a téléphoné de New York pour me proposer de le rejoindre. »*

**BILLY COX, NEW MUSICAL EXPRESS, DECEMBER 25, 1971**

**1963**

Initially helped by promoter "Gorgeous" George Odell, he begins securing regular live work as a backing musician on R&B package tours, including one headed by Sam Cooke and Jackie Wilson. Frequently leaving some treks and joining others, his apprenticeship is nationwide and includes additional work on the southern Chitlin' Circuit. In December, Hendrix also makes his vinyl debut on two Lonnie Youngblood singles recorded in Philadelphia.

Durch Vermittlung des Promoters „Gorgeous" George Odell schafft Jimi Hendrix es, regelmäßig Arbeit als Rhythmusgitarrist bei R&B-Tourneen zu bekommen; bei einer dieser Tourneen sind Sam Cooke und Jackie Wilson die Top Acts. Er steigt häufiger bei einer Tour aus und bei einer anderen wieder ein, verdient sich bei Backing-Auftritten im ganzen Land seine Sporen und ist auch auf dem „Chitlin' Circuit", in den schwarzen Musiktheatern, unterwegs. Im Dezember steht Jimi Hendrix zum ersten Mal im Plattenstudio, für zwei in Philadelphia aufgenommene Lonnie-Youngblood-Singles.

Grâce à l'agent « Gorgeous » George Odell, il est régulièrement engagé comme musicien de soutien pour une série de concerts Rhythm and Blues, dont une tournée dirigée par Sam Cooke and Jackie Wilson. Il enchaîne les périples, passe fréquemment d'un groupe à un autre, et parfait ainsi son apprentissage auprès des plus grands, notamment sur le « Chitlin' Circuit », dans le sud du pays. En décembre, Hendrix participe à sa première séance d'enregistrement pour deux 45 tours de Lonnie Youngblood, à Philadelphie.

## MARCH, 1964

Having relocated to the Hotel Theresa in Harlem, New York during the winter, Hendrix meets with the Isley Brothers through their friend, Tony Rice, to discuss joining their band for a North American tour. During the spring he will also record *Testify*, the first of several sides for the Isleys. Other New York studio work during the year will include two singles for Don Covay & the Goodtimers, while his increasingly in-demand live work includes further stints with Sam Cooke and Little Richard.

Im Winter ist Jimi Hendrix in das Hotel Theresa in Harlem, New York, gezogen, wo er die Isley Brothers durch den gemeinsamen Freund Tony Rice kennenlernt und eine gemeinsame Nordamerika-Tour anregt. Im Frühjahr spielt er *Testify*, die erste von mehreren Scheiben zusammen mit den Isleys. Außerdem entstehen in New York im Studio in diesem Jahr zwei Singles für Don Covay & the Goodtimers; auch für Live-Auftritte wird er immer häufiger angefragter, z. B. bei Konzerten von Sam Cooke und Little Richard.

À New York, Hendrix s'est installé à l'Hôtel Theresa de Harlem. Par l'intermédiaire de leur ami commun Tony Rice, il rencontre les Isley Brothers, qui l'engagent pour leur prochaine tournée nord-américaine. Au printemps, il collabore avec eux sur *Testify*, premier d'une série de disques qu'il enregistrera avec le groupe. Il décroche d'autres contrats comme musicien de studio à New York pendant l'année, notamment pour deux 45 tours de Don Covay & the Goodtimers, et remporte aussi un succès croissant sur scène, notamment avec Sam Cooke et Little Richard.

*"Just in case about three to four months from now you might hear a record by me which sounds terrible, don't feel ashamed, just wait until the money rolls in."*

„In drei bis vier Monaten wirst du vielleicht eine Platte von mir hören, die ganz furchtbar klingt. Bitte schäm dich nicht deswegen, die Dollars werden fließen."

« Juste au cas où d'ici trois ou quatre mois tu entendrais un disque de moi qui te paraîtrait atroce, n'aies pas honte, contente-toi d'attendre que l'argent tombe. »

**JIMI HENDRIX, IN A LETTER TO HIS FATHER, AUGUST 8, 1965**

© Christie's

## 1965

Hendrix spends much of the year flitting between Tennessee, Texas, California and New York playing gigs for the Isleys (with whom he records more studio tracks), Little Richard, King Curtis and Joey Dee & the Starliters, also recording *My Diary* with Rosa Lee Brooks while in Los Angeles. (Despite an urban legend to the contrary – perpetuated by his own later reminiscence – it's highly unlikely that he played in the backing band for Ike & Tina Turner, a rumor firmly denied by Tina.) He also makes his first television appearance, playing guitar in the backing band on *Shotgun* for R&B duo, Buddy & Stacy on Nashville's WLAC-TV Channel 5 show "Night Train" in July.

Jimi Hendrix verbringt das Jahr zum größten Teil unterwegs zwischen Tennessee, Texas, Kalifornien und New York, wo er für die Isleys (mit denen er noch weitere Stücke im Studio aufnimmt), Little Richard, King Curtis und Joey Dee & the Starliters auftritt und bei einem Aufenthalt in Los Angeles *My Diary* mit Rosa Lee Brooks einspielt. (Die Legende hält sich zwar hartnäckig – verstärkt durch seine eigenen Erinnerungen –,

er habe Rhythmusgitarre für Ike & Tina Turner gespielt, doch von Tina wird dies entschieden abgestritten.) Er hat im Juli seinen ersten Fernsehauftritt als Begleitmusiker des R&B-Duos Buddy & Stacy. Sie spielen in der Sendung „Night Train" auf Sender WLAC-TV Channel 5 in Nashville das Stück *Shotgun*.

Hendrix passe une majeure partie de l'année à papillonner entre Tennessee, Texas, Californie et New York pour une série de concerts avec les frères Isley (pour lesquels il enregistre aussi de nouveaux titres en studio), Little Richard, King Curtis, et Joey Dee & the Starliters ; il profite d'un passage à Los Angeles pour enregistrer *My Diary* avec Rosa Lee Brooks. Contrairement à la légende qui a couru ensuite, il est fort peu probable qu'il ait fait partie du groupe qui accompagnait Ike et Tina Turner (une rumeur entretenue par lui-même, et fermement démentie par Tina). En juillet, il apparaît pour la première fois à la télévision dans l'émission « Night Train » diffusée sur une chaîne locale de Nashville, WLAC-TV, comme guitariste, sur le morceau *Shotgun* du duo Buddy & Stacy.

**FRIDAY, OCTOBER 15, 1965**

Having recently begun session work for R&B band-leader, Curtis Knight in New York, Hendrix signs a three-year recording contract with producer Ed Chalpin, head of P.P.X. Enterprises, receiving $1 and a guarantee of a 1% royalty on records he is currently recording with Knight. (Chalpin will enforce this agreement on post-fame Hendrix collaborations with Knight recorded in 1967, and will also cause continued litigation problems for Hendrix and major record labels for many years.) His studio work over the next six months will also include sessions for Ray Sharpe, the Icemen and the King Curtis Orchestra.

Jimi Hendrix hat vor Kurzem als Sessionmusiker für den R&B-Bandleader Curtis Knight in New York angefangen und unterschreibt jetzt einen dreijährigen Plattenvertrag mit dem Produzenten Ed Chalpin, Chef von P.P.X. Enterprises. Er bekommt einen Dollar und eine garantierte Tantieme von 1% auf alle Platten, die er derzeit mit Curtis Knight zusammen aufnimmt. Chalpin wendet diesen Vertrag später auch auf die Hendrix-Zusammenarbeit mit Knight nach seinem großen Durchbruch 1967 an und überzieht ihn und seine großen Plattenlabels noch jahrelang mit kontinuierlichen Schadensersatzklagen. Als Studiomusiker arbeitet Jimi Hendrix in den nächsten sechs Monaten auch für Ray Sharpe, die Icemen, das King Curtis Orchestra u.a.

Alors qu'il vient d'entamer une collaboration en studio à New York avec Curtis Knight, le chef de file du Rhythm and Blues, Hendrix signe un contrat d'enregistrement exclusif de trois ans avec le producteur Ed Chalpin, le patron des studios P.P.X., qui prévoit un salaire symbolique d'un dollar assorti de 1% des droits d'auteurs en train d'enregistrer avec Knight. (Chalpin profitera de ces conditions scandaleusement avantageuses pour faire revenir Hendrix en studio avec Knight en 1967, alors qu'il est déjà connu, et elles poseront pendant plusieurs années d'épineux problèmes à Hendrix dans ses rapports avec les grandes maisons de disques.) Au cours des six mois suivants, il collabore aussi avec Ray Sharpe, les Icemen et le King Curtis Orchestra.

*"The man was happy to sign it. He knew that no backup musician ever gets a royalty ...*
*He was so happy to be an artist on his own right, he would have signed anything."*

*„Der Mann hat den Vertrag sehr gern unterschrieben. Er wusste, dass kein Begleitmusiker jemals*
*Tantiemen bekommt ... Er war so glücklich, endlich selbst als Künstler ernst genommen zu werden,*
*er hätte alles unterschrieben."*

*« Il était content de signer. Il savait qu'aucun musicien de studio ne reçoit de droits d'auteur. Il était*
*si heureux d'être considéré comme un artiste à part entière qu'il aurait signé n'importe quoi. »*

**ED CHALPIN**

# 1966

"We call it 'Electric Church Music'
because to us music is a religion."

„Wir nennen es ‚Electric Church Music' (‚Musik der elektrischen Kirche'),
weil Musik für uns Religion ist."

«Nous l'appelons ‹musique d'église électrique›
parce que pour nous la musique est une religion.»

**JIMI HENDRIX**

### THURSDAY, MAY 5, 1966

Hendrix backs Wilson Pickett, Percy Sledge and Esther Phillips at a party at the Prelude Club, in New York to celebrate the launch of Sledge's new album.

Jimi Hendrix spielt für Wilson Pickett, Percy Sledge und Esther Phillips bei einer Party im Prelude Club in New York, bei der das neue Sledge-Album vorgestellt wird.

Hendrix joue en soutien à Wilson Pickett, Percy Sledge et Esther Phillips lors d'une soirée au Prelude Club, à New York, pour la sortie du nouvel album de Sledge.

### FRIDAY, MAY 13, 1966

Curtis Knight & the Squires begin a two-week stint at the Cheetah Club in New York, their shirts designed to match the fabric of the venue's couches and walls. Hendrix quits the residency after one week.

Curtis Knight & the Squires spielen zwei Wochen lang im Cheetah Club in New York, alle in Hemden, die zu den Sofas und Stofftapeten des Clubs passen. Jimi Hendrix steigt nach einer Woche aus.

Curtis Knight & the Squires entament une session de deux semaines au Cheetah Club de New York ; leurs chemises panthère sont assorties aux fauteuils et aux murs de la salle. Hendrix s'en va au bout d'une semaine.

### WEDNESDAY, JUNE 1, 1966

Hendrix forms his own group, Jimmy James & the Blue Flames, which plays a mix of R&B standards and original material. A fluid group, which at times features Randy Wolfe (subsequently known as Randy California) and Jeff Baxter, will eventually head to Greenwich Village, gigging regularly at the Cafe Wha?

Jimi Hendrix gründet seine erste eigene Band namens Jimmy James & the Blue Flames, die eine Mischung aus R&B-Standards und Originalmaterial spielt. Die Gruppe, zu deren veränderlicher Besetzung manchmal auch Randy Wolfe (später bekannt als

Randy California) und Jeff Baxter gehören, schafft es ins Greenwich Village, wo sie regelmäßig im Cafe Wha? auftritt.

Hendrix forme son propre groupe, Jimmy James & the Blue Flames, dont le répertoire mélange standards du Rhythm and Blues et compositions originales. Ce groupe à géométrie variable, qui compte parfois Randy Wolfe (ensuite connu sous le nom de Randy California) et Jeff Baxter, prend ses quartiers à Greenwich Village, où il se produit régulièrement au Cafe Wha?

### WEDNESDAY, AUGUST 3, 1966

On the recommendation of Keith Richard's girlfriend, Linda Keith, Animals' bassist Chas Chandler—who is finishing a six-week US tour with his band but looking for emerging talent to produce and manage—sees Hendrix play at the Café Wha? and suggests that he should relocate to London.

Auf Empfehlung von Keith Richards Freundin Linda Keith geht der Bassist der Animals, Chas Chandler, ins Café Wha? und hört sich Jimi Hendrix an. Chandler hat gerade eine sechswöchige US-Tournee mit seiner Band beendet und sucht nun nach jungen Talenten, die er produzieren und managen kann. Er schlägt Jimi Hendrix vor, nach London zu kommen.

Sur le conseil de la petite amie de Keith Richard, Linda Keith, le bassiste des Animals Chas Chandler, qui termine une tournée américaine de six semaines et recherche de jeunes talents, voit Hendrix jouer au Cafe Wha?; il lui suggère de s'installer à Londres.

**FRIDAY, SEPTEMBER 23, 1966**

With a passport (number G1044108) issued just hours earlier, Hendrix and Chandler fly first class from Kennedy International Airport in New York to London's Heathrow. (Legend has it that on the flight Hendrix decides to change the spelling of his name from Jimmy to Jimi.) On arrival, Hendrix—without a work permit—initially has trouble entering the country. He checks into the Hyde Park Towers Hotel in Inverness Terrace, and later jams at the Scotch of St. James nightclub.

Mit einem nur wenige Stunden zuvor ausgestellten Reisepass (Nummer G1044108) fliegen Jimi Hendrix und Chas Chandler erster Klasse vom Kennedy International Airport in New York nach London-Heathrow. (Der Legende nach beschließt Jimi Hendrix auf dem Flug, die Schreibweise seines Vornamens von Jimmy in

Jimi zu ändern.) Bei der Ankunft hat er ohne Arbeitserlaubnis erst einmal Schwierigkeiten bei der Einreise. Jimi Hendrix mietet sich im Hyde Park Towers Hotel in Inverness Terrace ein und jammt später im Nachtclub Scotch of St. James.

Grâce à un passeport (numéro G1044108) émis seulement quelques heures auparavant, Hendrix s'envole en première classe de l'aéroport international JFK de New York avec Chandler et atterrit à Londres. (Ce serait pendant ce vol que Hendrix aurait décidé de changer l'orthographe de son prénom en Jimi.) Hendrix n'a pas de permis de travail et a du mal à entrer sur le territoire britannique, mais il s'installe finalement au Hyde Park Towers Hotel à Inverness Terrace et se produit bientôt dans la boîte de nuit Scotch of St. James.

*"I said I might as well go because nothing much was happening. We were making something near $3 a night, and you know we were starving."*

*„Ich habe gesagt, ich könnte wirklich auch nach London gehen, weil sich sowieso nicht viel getan hat. Wir haben zirka drei Dollar pro Abend verdient und waren praktisch am Verhungern."*

*« Je me suis dit que je ferais aussi bien d'y aller parce qu'il ne se passait pas grand-chose pour moi à ce moment-là. On ne se faisait que dans les trois dollars par soir et on mangeait rarement à notre faim. »*

**JIMI HENDRIX, DOWNBEAT, APRIL 4, 1968**

*"I was half convinced to sign him up before I even heard him play. We had a talk in a little restaurant before he played at the club—I remember thinking 'this cat's wild enough to upset more people than Jagger!' ... By the time I heard him play Wild Thing and Like A Rolling Stone I was certain and when he did a version of Hey Joe that clinched it."*

*„Ich war schon halb entschlossen, ihn unter Vertrag zu nehmen, bevor ich ihn überhaupt spielen gehört hatte. Vor seinem Auftritt im Club unterhielten wir uns in einem kleinen Restaurant - und ich weiß noch, wie ich dachte: ‚Der Typ ist so wild, über den werden sich die Leute mehr aufregen als über Jagger!' ... Als er dann Wild Thing und Like A Rolling Stone spielte, war ich mir ziemlich sicher, und als er eine Version von Hey Joe spielte, war die Sache für mich völlig klar."*

*« J'étais déjà à moitié convaincu avant-même de l'entendre jouer. Nous avons discuté dans un petit restaurant avant d'aller au club et je me souviens de m'être dit : "Ce chat-là est suffisamment sauvage pour énerver encore plus de gens que Jagger !" [...] Après l'avoir entendu jouer Wild Thing et Like A Rolling Stone j'étais sûr que ça vaudrait le coup, et quand il a fait sa reprise de Hey Joe, j'ai pris ma décision. »*

**CHAS CHANDLER, NEW MUSICAL EXPRESS, NOVEMBER 16, 1968**

### THURSDAY, SEPTEMBER 29, 1966

Noel Redding, turning up yesterday to audition as a guitarist for the Animals, meets Hendrix for the first time at Birdland off Jermyn Street. With Chandler lending Redding his bass guitar and Mike O'Neill of Nero & the Gladiators on piano and Aynsley Dunbar on drums, the quartet jams with a view to becoming the Jimi Hendrix Experience—the named coined by the Animals' manager, Mike Jeffery.

Noel Redding, der am Vortag als Gitarrist bei den Animals vorgespielt hat, lernt Jimi Hendrix im Birdland an der Jermyn Street kennen. Chas Chandler leiht Noel Redding seinen Bass aus, Mike O'Neill von Nero & The Gladiators spielt Klavier und Aynsley Dunbar

Schlagzeug. Das Quartett jammt zum ersten Mal zusammen, kurz darauf ist The Jimi Hendrix Experience gegründet – der Name stammt vom Manager der Animals, Mike Jeffery.

Noel Redding, qui a auditionné la veille pour devenir le nouveau guitariste des Animals, rencontre Hendrix pour la première fois chez Birdland, sur Jermyn Street. Chandler prête sa basse à Redding, Mike O'Neill, des Nero & The Gladiators, se met au piano et Aynsley Dunbar à la batterie, et ce quatuor improvisé commence à jouer ensemble. Ils deviennent le Jimi Hendrix Experience, un nom trouvé par le manager des Animals, Mike Jeffery.

## SATURDAY, OCTOBER 1, 1966

Introduced to Eric Clapton by Chandler, Hendrix jams with Clapton's new group Cream at Central London Polytechnic in Regent Street, London on *Killing Floor*. They will remain firm friends until Hendrix's death.

Chas Chandler macht Jimi Hendrix mit Eric Clapton bekannt. Beim Auftritt von Eric Claptons neuer Gruppe Cream im Central London Polytechnic in der Regent Street in London spielt er bei dem Stück *Killing Floor* mit. Die beiden bleiben bis zu Jimi Hendrixs Tod enge Freunde.

Eric Clapton - que Chandler a présenté à Hendrix - l'invite à rejoindre son nouveau groupe Cream sur la scène de l'université polytechnique de Londres, sur Regent Street, pour *Killing Floor*. Ils resteront des amis proches jusqu'à la mort de Hendrix.

*"After Jimi's pyrotechnical performance, EC was absolutely deflated emotionally and uncharacteristically left the gig in a taxi with me and another roommate. During the ten-minute ride back to our flat he lay on the floor of the taxi and literally moaned in misery. He thought his career was over."*

*„Nach Jimis Feuerwerk von einem Auftritt war EC völlig am Boden zerstört und verließ den Gig ganz untypisch mit mir und einer Mitbewohnerin zusammen im Taxi. Während der zehnminütigen Fahrt zu unserer Wohnung lag er im Taxi auf dem Boden und stöhnte elendiglich vor sich hin. Er war überzeugt, dass seine Karriere am Ende war."*

*« Après la performance pyrotechnique de Hendrix, EC était complètement défait et, fait très exceptionnel, il est rentré à la maison en taxi avec moi et un autre ami. Il a passé les dix minutes du trajet couché sur le plancher de la voiture à gémir de désespoir. Il pensait que sa carrière était finie. »*

**BETSY FOWLER**

### WEDNESDAY, OCTOBER 5, 1966

Having parted ways three days ago with George Fame & the Blue Flames, drummer Mitch Mitchell auditions for the Jimi Hendrix Experience at Les Cousins. Mitchell joins after Aynsley Dunbar and John Banks both pass on the offer.

Le batteur Mitch Mitchell, qui a quitté trois jours plus tôt George Fame & the Blue Flames, passe une audition chez Les Cousins pour se joindre au Jimi Hendrix Experience. Il est choisi après le refus d'Aynsley Dunbar et de John Banks.

Nachdem Drummer Mitch Mitchell drei Tage zuvor George Fame & the Blue Flames verlassen hat, spielt er im Les Cousins bei The Jimi Hendrix Experience vor. Mitchell steigt ein, nachdem Aynsley Dunbar und John Banks abgelehnt haben.

*"Chas said there was a gig in Paris the next week with Johnny Hallyday and asked if we fancied doing it. So I said 'OK'."*

*„Chas meinte, es gäbe in der nächsten Woche einen Gig in Paris mit Johnny Hallyday und fragte, ob wir da vielleicht spielen wollen. Ich sagte: ‚Warum nicht.'"*

*« Chas a dit qu'il y avait un concert à Paris la semaine suivante avec Johnny Hallyday et m'a demandé si ça me plairait d'y participer. Alors j'ai dit "OK". »*

**MITCH MITCHELL**

**TUESDAY, OCTOBER 11, 1966**
After rehearsing for several days together, the trio signs a management and publishing deal with Jeffery's ANIM Management company.

Das Trio hat mehrere Tage lang geprobt und unterschreibt einen Management- und Veröffentlichungsvertrag mit Mike Jefferys Managementfirma ANIM.

Après plusieurs jours de répétitions, le trio signe un contrat de promotion et de diffusion avec la compagnie de Jeffery, ANIM Management.

"Johnny Hallyday's latest discovery was a singer and guitar player with bushy hair, a bad mixture of James Brown and Chuck Berry, who pulled a wry face onstage for a quarter of an hour and also played with his teeth."

„Johnny Hallydays neuste Entdeckung war ein Sänger und Gitarrenspieler mit struppigem Kraushaar, eine unerfreuliche Mischung aus James Brown und Chuck Berry, der eine Viertelstunde lang auf der Bühne Verrenkungen machte und mit den Zähnen spielte."

« La dernière "découverte" de Johnny Hallyday [est] un chanteur guitariste à la chevelure broussailleuse, mauvais cocktail de James Brown et de Chuck Berry, qui se contorsionne pendant un bon quart d'heure sur la scène en jouant parfois de la guitare avec les dents. »

**L'EURE ECLAIR, OCTOBER 14, 1966**

### THURSDAY, OCTOBER 13, 1966

The Jimi Hendrix Experience makes its live debut at the Novelty in Évreux, France, opening for French singer, Johnny Hallyday. The four-date tour will climax with an appearance at the Paris Olympia on Tuesday. Hallyday had seen Hendrix sit in with Brian Auger at Blaises Club two weeks ago in London.

The Jimi Hendrix Experience haben ihren ersten Live-Auftritt im Novelty-Kinotheater in Évreux in Frankreich, wo sie als Vorband für den französischen Sänger Johnny Hallyday spielen. Die vier Konzerte finden ihren Höhepunkt am Dienstag im Pariser Olympia. Johnny Hallyday hatte Jimi Hendrix zwei Wochen zuvor bei einer Jamsession mit Brian Auger im Blaises Club in London gesehen.

Le Jimi Hendrix Experience fait ses débuts sur scène au Novelty d'Évreux en première partie de Johnny Hallyday. La tournée de quatre dates s'achève en apothéose à l'Olympia de Paris, le mardi. Hallyday est allé écouter Hendrix avec Brian Auger au Blaises Club de Londres deux semaines plus tôt.

## SUNDAY, OCTOBER 23, 1966

Having returned from France, the Jimi Hendrix
Experience records for the first time, at De Lane Lea
Studios in London, cutting *Hey Joe* and *Stone Free—*
both of which will become revered songs in the Hendrix canon. (Initially, the England-based Hendrix will
find greater respect and success in Britain, where *Hey
Joe* will open his United Kingdom chart account in
January, a full eight months before his home country
takes notice.)

Nach der Rückkehr aus Frankreich gehen The Jimi
Hendrix Experience zu ersten Aufnahmen in die De
Lane Lea Studios in London, wo sie *Hey Joe* und *Stone
Free* einspielen – beide werden zu legendären Songs
im Hendrix-Repertoire. Anfangs genießt der in England
lebende Jimi Hendrix dort weitaus größeren Erfolg
und Respekt als in den USA – *Hey Joe* schafft es im
Januar erstmals in die britischen Charts, während sein
Heimatland erst geschlagene acht Monate später
Notiz von dem Song nimmt.

De retour à Londres, le Jimi Hendrix Experience
entre en studio pour la première fois chez De Lane
Lea, et enregistre *Hey Joe* et *Stone Free*, deux titres
révérés par les fans de Hendrix. (Au départ, il rencontre plus de respect et de succès au Royaume-Uni,
où *Hey Joe* entre dans le classement des meilleures
ventes en janvier, huit mois avant que son propre pays
remarque sa sortie.)

**TUESDAY, OCTOBER 25, 1966**
The Experience performs a private showcase at the Scotch of St. James club, with Paul McCartney among the impressed attendees.

The Experience spielen bei einem privaten Showcase im Scotch of St. James Club. Zu den beeindruckten Zuhörern zählt auch Paul McCartney.

L'Experience donne un concert privé au club Scotch of St. James, devant un public enthousiaste qui compte Paul McCartney.

**SATURDAY, OCTOBER 29, 1966**
With word-of-mouth quickly spreading, **Record Mirror** reports that "Chas Chandler has signed and brought to this country a 20-year-old Negro called Jim Hendrix who—among other things—plays the guitar with his teeth and is being hailed in some quarters as a main contender for the title of 'next big thing'."

Jimi Hendrixs sensationelle Fähigkeiten sprechen sich schnell herum, und der **Record Mirror** berichtet: „Chas Chandler hat einen zwanzigjährigen Schwarzen namens Jim Hendrix unter Vertrag genommen und in dieses Land gebracht, der – unter anderem – mit den Zähnen Gitarre spielt und in gewissen Kreisen als bester Anwärter auf ‚das nächste große Ding' gilt."

Le bouche-à-oreille fait son œuvre et le **Record Mirror** annonce que « Chas Chandler a signé et ramené dans ce pays un Noir de 20 ans appelé Jim Hendrix qui – entre autres choses – joue de la guitare avec les dents et que beaucoup considèrent, dans certains lieux, comme le "le prochain génie du rock" ».

**TUESDAY, NOVEMBER 8, TO FRIDAY, NOVEMBER 11, 1966**
On its second visit to the continent, the Experience plays eight gigs over four nights at the Big Apple club, Munich, West Germany, for which the trio is paid £300. During the opening night performance Hendrix is pulled offstage by enthusiastic fans.

The Experience spielen bei ihrem zweiten Besuch auf dem Kontinent im Laufe von vier Abenden achtmal im Big Apple Club in München und verdienen 300 Pfund. Am ersten Abend wird Jimi Hendrix von begeisterten Fans von der Bühne gerissen.

Au cours de son deuxième périple sur le continent, l'Experience donne huit concerts en quatre soirs au Big Apple de Munich, en Allemagne de l'Ouest ; ils touchent un cachet de 300 livres sterling. Dès le premier soir, Hendrix est tiré dans la fosse par ses fans en liesse.

### FRIDAY, NOVEMBER 25, 1966

The press is introduced to the Jimi Hendrix Experience, when the trio performs at a media showcase at the Bag O' Nails club in London. Among the attendant celebrities—John Lennon, Paul McCartney, Eric Clapton, Pete Townshend and Jimmy Page. Their first British interview, with **Record Mirror**'s Peter Jones, will appear in the paper's December 10 issue.

The Jimi Hendrix Experience stellen sich der Presse bei einem Medien-Showcase im Bag O' Nails Club in London vor. Viele berühmte Musiker sind im Publikum – John Lennon, Paul McCartney, Eric Clapton, Pete Townshend und Jimmy Page. Das erste Interview in England, mit Peter Jones, erscheint in der Ausgabe des **Record Mirror** vom 10. Dezember.

Un concert est organisé au club Bag O' Nails de Londres pour présenter le Jimi Hendrix Experience à la presse. Parmi les invités figurent aussi des célébrités du monde musical : John Lennon, Paul McCartney, Eric Clapton, Pete Townshend et Jimmy Page. Ils accordent leur première interview britannique à Peter Jones, du **Record Mirror**, qui paraît dans l'édition du 10 décembre.

*"I had six guitars and I sold five of them to pay for (the) reception."*

*„Ich hatte sechs Gitarren und musste fünf davon verkaufen, um für den Empfang zu bezahlen."*

*« J'avais six guitares et j'en ai vendu cinq pour payer cette réception. »*

**CHAS CHANDLER**

© Christie's

### THURSDAY, DECEMBER 1, 1966

Hendrix signs an exclusive four-year management deal with Yameta, a Bahamian offshore company owned by Mike Jeffery and Who managers, Kit Lambert and Chris Stamp.

Jimi Hendrix unterschreibt einen vierjährigen Exklusiv-Managementvertrag mit Yameta, einer Briefkastenfirma auf den Bahamas, die Mike Jeffery und den Managern von The Who Kit Lambert und Chris Stamp gehört.

Hendrix signe un contrat d'exclusivité de quatre ans avec Yameta, une compagnie offshore bahaméenne appartenant à Mike Jeffery et aux agents des Who, Kit Lambert et Chris Stamp.

*"Jimi has great stage presence and an exceptional guitar technique which involved playing with his teeth on many occasions and no hands at all on others. Jimi looks like becoming one of the big club names of '67."*

*„Jimi hat eine fantastische Bühnenpräsenz und eine herausragende Technik. Er spielt die Gitarre wiederholt mit den Zähnen oder ganz ohne Hände. Es sieht so aus, als ob Jimi 1967 einer der ganz großen Namen in der Clubszene wird."*

*« Jimi a une grande présence sur scène et une technique de guitare exceptionnelle qui lui permet de jouer avec ses dents, et parfois sans utiliser ses mains du tout. Jimi est sur le point de devenir un des grands noms de l'année 1967. »*

**CHRIS WELCH, MELODY MAKER, DECEMBER 31, 1966**

### FRIDAY, DECEMBER 16, 1966

Recorded three days ago, "Ready Steady Go!" airs on ITV with the Jimi Hendrix Experience making its first television appearance, as its debut single, a cover of the Leaves hit (although Hendrix prefers Tim Rose's version) *Hey Joe*, is released on Polydor Records, after being rejected by Decca.

„Ready Steady Go!" wurde drei Tage zuvor aufgenommen und läuft auf ITV. Es ist der erste Fernsehauftritt der Jimi Hendrix Experience. Gleichzeitig kommt ihre erste Single bei Polydor Records heraus, nachdem sie von Decca abgelehnt wurde: *Hey Joe*, Coverversion eines Hits der Leaves (Jimi Hendrix bevorzugt allerdings Tim Roses Version.)

Enregistrée trois jours plus tôt, l'émission « Ready Steady Go! » est diffusée sur ITV avec pour la première fois à l'écran le Jimi Hendrix Experience, qui joue son 45 tours, la reprise du tube des Leaves *Hey Joe* (Hendrix préfère d'ailleurs la version de Tim Rose). Le disque vient de sortir chez Polydor après avoir été refusé par Decca.

**WEDNESDAY, DECEMBER 21, 1966**

The Experience plays at Blaises Club in Queensgate, London in front of a duly-impressed star-packed crowd, performing five numbers: *Rock Me Baby, Third Stone From The Sun, Like A Rolling Stone, Hey Joe* and *Wild Thing.*

L'Experience se produit au Blaises Club de Queensgate, à Londres, devant un public truffé de vedettes et conquis. Le trio joue *Rock Me Baby, Third Stone From The Sun, Like A Rolling Stone, Hey Joe* et *Wild Thing.*

The Experience spielen fünf Stücke vor einem begeisterten, mit Prominenz gefüllten Publikum im Blaises Club in Queensgate, London: *Rock Me Baby, Third Stone From The Sun, Like A Rolling Stone, Hey Joe* und *Wild Thing.*

**MONDAY, DECEMBER 26, 1966**
Hendrix writes *Purple Haze* in the dressing room, while waiting to go onstage, at The Upper Cut club in South London.

Jimi Hendrix schreibt *Purple Haze* in der Garderobe des Upper Cut Club in South London, während er auf seinen Auftritt wartet.

Hendrix compose *Purple Haze* dans sa loge du club The Upper Cut, dans le sud de Londres, alors qu'il attend de passer sur scène.

**THURSDAY, DECEMBER 29, 1966**
The trio performs *Hey Joe*—currently in its first week on the British chart at No. 38 on its way to a No. 3 peak—on BBC1-TV's "Top Of The Pops."

Das Trio spielt *Hey Joe* – derzeit in der ersten Chartwoche auf dem 38. Platz und auf dem Weg zur Höchstplatzierung auf Platz 3 – in der Sendung „Top Of The Pops" auf BBC1.

Le trio joue *Hey Joe* dans l'émission culte de la BBC1, « Top Of The Pops ». Le titre vient d'entrer à la 38ᵉ place des meilleures ventes britanniques, et deviendra numéro trois.

# 1967

*"The time I burned my guitar it was like a sacrifice.
You sacrifice the things you love. I love my guitar."*

*„Das war eine Art Opfer, als ich meine Gitarre verbrannt habe.
Man opfert die Dinge, die man liebt. Ich liebe meine Gitarre."*

*« La fois où j'ai brûlé ma guitare, c'était comme un sacrifice.
On sacrifie les choses qu'on aime. J'aime ma guitare. »*

**JIMI HENDRIX**

**WEDNESDAY, JANUARY 11, 1967**

During a busy schedule of gigs and recording sessions, the Experience records *Purple Haze, 51st Anniversary* and *Third Stone From The Sun* at De Lane Lea Studios before playing two evening shows across town at the Bag O' Nails club.

The Experience haben einen vollen Terminkalender mit vielen Auftritten und Studioterminen und nehmen *Purple Haze, 51st Anniversary* und *Third Stone From* *The Sun* in den De Lane Lea Studios auf. Am gleichen Abend bestreiten sie noch zwei Auftritte im Bag O' Nails Club auf der anderen Seite von London.

L'agenda du groupe est complet. Ce dernier enregistre *Purple Haze, 51st Anniversary* et *Third Stone From The Sun* aux studios De Lane Lea et, le soir même, donne deux concerts au Bag O' Nails à l'autre bout de la ville.

### TUESDAY, JANUARY 24, 1967

A record-breaking 1,400 people cram into the Marquee in London's West End to see the Experience perform *Hey Joe*, *Stone Free*, *Like A Rolling Stone* and *Wild Thing*.

Rekordverdächtige 1.400 Zuschauer drängeln sich im Marquee im Londoner West End, wo The Experience *Hey Joe*, *Stone Free*, *Like A Rolling Stone* und *Wild Thing* spielen.

Quelque 1 400 personnes, un record, se pressent au Marquee, dans le quartier londonien de West End, pour écouter l'Experience jouer *Hey Joe*, *Stone Free*, *Like A Rolling Stone* et *Wild Thing*.

© Hard Rock Cafe

**SUNDAY, JANUARY 29, 1967**

Performing live almost daily throughout the month, the band appears at London's Saville Theatre on a bill with the Koobas, Thoughts and headliners, the Who.

Die Band tritt den ganzen Monat lang fast täglich auf, u.a. im Londoner Saville Theatre zusammen mit den Koobas und Thoughts, Headliner sind The Who.

Le trio, qui a joué quasiment tous les soirs du mois, se produit au Saville Theatre. Il partage l'affiche avec les Koobas, les Thoughts et les Who.

*"The most obvious thing about Jimi Hendrix is that he is not pretty—neither is his raw, exciting brand of beat music."*

*„Jimi Hendrix ist ganz offensichtlich nicht hübsch - genauso wenig wie seine aufregende, rohe Beatmusik."*

*« Ce qui est le plus frappant à propos de Jimi Hendrix, c'est qu'il n'est pas "joli" - et sa beat music crue, excitante, ne l'est pas non plus. »*

**JOHN KING, NEW MUSICAL EXPRESS, JANUARY 28, 1967**

### THURSDAY, MARCH 2, 1967

Following a gig supporting Soft Machine at London's Roundhouse—where Hendrix has his guitar stolen—the Experience now performs for the weekly German TV show "The Beat Club," live from the Marquee Club in Wardour Street.

Nach einem Gig mit Soft Machine im Londoner Roundhouse – wo Jimi Hendrix die Gitarre gestohlen wird – spielen The Experience an diesem Tag für die allwöchentliche deutsche Fernsehsendung „Beat-Club" und werden live aus dem Marquee Club in der Wardour Street zugeschaltet.

Après un concert de soutien à Soft Machine au Roundhouse de Londres, où Hendrix se fait voler sa guitare, l'Experience participe à l'émission hebdomadaire « The Beat Club » en direct du Marquee, sur Wardour Street.

### TUESDAY, MARCH 14, 1967

Mike Jeffery signs the group to a five-year, $1-million recording deal with Reprise Records in the United States. Warner-Reprise's president Mo Austin describes it as the highest fee the company has ever paid for a new artist.

Mike Jeffery schließt für die Gruppe einen Plattenvertrag mit Reprise Records in den USA über eine Million Dollar für fünf Jahre ab. Warner-Reprise-Chef Mo Austin sagt, es sei die höchste Gage, die von der Plattenfirma je an einen neuen Künstler bezahlt worden sei.

Mike Jeffery fait signer au groupe un contrat d'enregistrement de cinq ans pour un million de dollars avec la maison de disques américaine Reprise Records. Le président de Warner-Reprise, Mo Austin, l'annonce comme le plus lucratif jamais accordé à un artiste débutant.

*"We shall introduce a completely new conception in promotion which should put Jimi right at the top in a very short time."*

*„Wir werden ein völlig neues Werbekonzept einführen, mit dem Jimi in kürzester Zeit ganz oben landen dürfte."*

*« Nous allons mettre en place un tout nouveau type de promotion qui devrait très rapidement propulser Jimi au sommet. »*

**A REPRISE SPOKESMAN**

## THURSDAY, MARCH 30, 1967

During an appearance on BBC1-TV's "Top Of The Pops"—at which artists mime to their hits—a technician inadvertently puts on the backing track of Alan Price's *Simon Smith And His Amazing Dancing Bear* instead of *Purple Haze*, to which Hendrix responds, "I don't know the words to that one, man."

Bei einem BBC-Fernsehauftritt in „Top Of The Pops" - für den Playback eingesetzt wird - legt ein Techniker versehentlich die Begleitmusik von Alan Prices *Simon Smith And His Amazing Dancing Bear* statt *Purple Haze* auf, worauf Jimi Hendrix meint: „Von dem Stück kenne ich den Text nicht, Mann."

Hendrix est invité à l'émission de la BBC1 « Top Of The Pops », au cours de laquelle les artistes doivent mimer leurs chansons. Un technicien lance par erreur la chanson d'Alan Price, *Simon Smith And His Amazing Dancing Bear*, au lieu de *Purple Haze*, et Hendrix s'exclame : « Celle-là, je connais pas les paroles, mec. »

Purple Haze—"Mean, insidious, cloying r-and-b—the sort of stuff we rarely hear produced in this country."

Purple Haze - „Fieser, hinterhältiger, widerlicher R&B - die Art Zeug, die wir hier in diesem Land viel zu selten zu hören kriegen."

Purple Haze, « du R&B mesquin, insidieux, repoussant, comme on en produit rarement dans ce pays. »

**DEREK JOHNSON, NEW MUSICAL EXPRESS, MARCH 25, 1967**

"After Jimi's performances on Saturday and Sunday night I was told that he had got to change his act. The tour organizers said he was too suggestive. I think this is a joke myself and there's not a chance of his changing his act."

„Nach Jimis Auftritt am Samstag und Sonntag wurde mir gesagt, er müsse seine Show ändern. Die Tourneeveranstalter meinten, er sei zu anzüglich. Ich persönlich finde das einen Witz; er wird seine Show niemals ändern."

« Après les performances de Jimi samedi et dimanche soir, on m'a dit qu'il devait faire quelques changements. Les organisateurs de la tournée trouvaient qu'il était trop suggestif. Personnellement, je prends ça pour une blague, et il n'y a aucune chance pour qu'il change quoi que ce soit à sa façon de jouer. »

**CHAS CHANDLER**

## FRIDAY, MARCH 31, 1967

The group begins its first British tour, a 25-date, twice-nightly package with the Walker Brothers, Cat Stevens and special guest star Engelbert Humperdinck, at the Astoria Theatre in Finsbury Park, London, set to end April 30 at the Granada Theatre in Tooting, London. On this first date Hendrix is taken to hospital after setting his guitar alight and suffering minor burns to his hands. (In addition to his guitar distortion and feedback stage devices, Hendrix will make a nightly habit of playing the instrument with his teeth, before setting fire to it on occasion. Rank Theatres warn Hendrix to tone down his act during the tour, prompting the response: "All I want to do is sing and play guitar. I'm bemused. I play the way I play and I can't understand the situation at all.")

Die Band geht zusammen mit den Walker Brothers, Cat Stevens und Engelbert Humperdinck als Special Guest auf die erste Tournee durch Großbritannien: 25 Auftritte, zwei Konzerte pro Abend. Die Tournee beginnt im Astoria Theatre in Finsbury Park, London, das Finale soll am 30. April im Granada Theatre in Tooting, London, stattfinden. Am ersten Abend muss Jimi Hendrix ins Krankenhaus gebracht werden, nachdem er seine Gitarre angezündet und leichte Verbrennungen an den Händen erlitten hat. (Jimi macht es sich zur Angewohnheit, nicht nur mit Verzerrung und Feedback zu arbeiten, sondern das Instrument auch allabendlich mit den Zähnen zu bearbeiten und hin und wieder abzufackeln. Die Rank Theatres warnen ihn, seinen Act auf der Tournee etwas zurückhaltender zu gestalten, woraufhin er erwidert: „Ich will nichts weiter als singen und Gitarre spielen. Ich bin irritiert. Ich spiele so, wie ich spiele, und ich verstehe überhaupt nicht, worin das Problem besteht.")

Le groupe entame sa première tournée britannique pour 25 dates à raison de deux concerts par soir au côté des Walker Brothers, de Cat Stevens et de l'invité d'honneur Engelbert Humperdinck, à l'Astoria Theatre de Finsbury Park (Londres). Elle doit se terminer le 30 avril au Granada Theatre de Tooting, également à Londres. Le premier soir, Hendrix est emmené à l'hôpital après s'être légèrement brûlé les mains en mettant le feu à sa guitare. (Les effets de distorsion et de larsen font alors autant partie du spectacle que son habitude de jouer avec les dents avant de mettre le feu à son instrument, et les salles Rank demandent à Hendrix de se calmer un peu pendant sa tournée. Hendrix leur fait cette réponse : « Tout ce que je veux, c'est chanter et jouer de la guitare. Je suis perplexe. Je joue comme je joue, et je ne comprends pas du tout où est le problème. »)

## FRIDAY, APRIL 7, 1967

During a gyrating performance at the ABC in Carlisle, Hendrix cuts his foot, requiring four stitches. The episode brings allegations that his set is "too provocative." Barry Clayman, the tour's co-promoter, says "The Hendrix Experience have toned down their act as requested by ourselves and by the Rank and ABC chains. The situation is now resolved." Chandler responds by saying that Hendrix's foot injury caused him to jump around somewhat which might have "prompted the suggestion that he was too sexy." Agent Dick Katz will comment: "It was all a publicity stunt—and it paid off."

Im ABC in Carlisle legt Jimi Hendrix eine besonders energiegeladene Bühnenshow hin, wobei er sich den Fuß verletzt. Nach dem Vorfall werden Stimmen laut, sein Auftritt sei „zu provozierend". Barry Clayman, einer der Tour-Promoter, erklärt: „Die Hendrix Experience nehmen sich jetzt, wie von uns und den Veranstaltern gewünscht, bei ihrem Auftritt zurück. Das Problem ist damit gelöst." Chas Chandler erwidert, Jimi Hendrix habe infolge seiner Fußverletzung vielleicht etwas herumspringen müssen, was „zur Andeutung geführt hat, er sei zu sexy." Agent Dick Katz: „Es war alles ein großer Werbegag – und der hat sich ausgezahlt."

Au cours d'une performance ébouriffante pour ABC à Carlisle, Hendrix se blesse au pied. Ce nouvel incident pousse certains à juger son jeu scénique « trop provocant ». Barry Clayman, coproducteur de la tournée, déclare : « Le Hendrix Experience a modéré son style comme nous-même, le Rank et ABC le lui avons demandé. Le problème est maintenant résolu. » Chandler renchérit en déclarant qu'à cause de sa blessure au pied, Hendrix s'est déhanché d'une manière qui « a pu être interprétée comme trop sensuelle ». L'agent Dick Katz estime quant à lui que « tout ça n'était qu'un coup de pub – très payant, d'ailleurs ».

"The Jimi Hendrix Experience are a musical labyrinth—you either find your way into the solid wall of incredible sound, or you sit back and gasp at Hendrix's guitar antics and showmanship, wondering what it's all about."

„The Jimi Hendrix Experience sind ein musikalisches Labyrinth - entweder findet man einen Weg hinein in diese dichte Wand unglaublicher Klänge, oder man lehnt sich zurück und staunt über Hendrix mit seiner irren Show und seinen Gitarrenmätzchen und fragt sich, was das alles bedeuten mag."

« Le Jimi Hendrix Experience est un labyrinthe musical - soit on trouve son chemin dans ce mur de son incroyable de densité, soit on reste assis bouche bée devant la maîtrise technique de Hendrix et ses talents d'homme de scène, à se demander ce qui se passe. »

**KEITH ALTHAM, NEW MUSICAL EXPRESS, APRIL 8, 1967**

### SUNDAY, MAY 7, 1967

Three months after making its debut at London's Saville Theatre, opening for the Who, the Experience now returns as headliners.

Drei Monate nachdem The Experience als Vorgruppe von The Who zum ersten Mal im Saville Theatre in London aufgetreten sind, kehren sie jetzt als Hauptband zurück.

Trois mois après ses débuts en première partie des Who, l'Experience retourne au Saville Theatre de Londres, cette fois en tête d'affiche.

*"If Eric Clapton's in the audience, can he come up here and tune this thing?"*

*„Falls Eric Clapton im Publikum ist: Könnte er hochkommen und das Ding hier stimmen?"*

*« Si Eric Clapton est dans la salle, est-ce qu'il pourrait monter ici pour accorder ce truc ? »*

**JIMI HENDRIX, MAY 7, 1967**

**TUESDAY, MAY 9, 1967**
Hendrix is a guest of honor at the Variety Club of Great Britain's "Tribute To The Recording Industry" annual Golden Disc luncheon at London's Dorchester Hotel.

Jimi Hendrix ist Ehrengast im Variety Club bei der alljährlichen Golden Disc Feier des britischen „Tribute To The Recording Industry" im Londoner Dorchester Hotel.

Hendrix fait partie des invités d'honneur de l'hommage annuel à l'industrie du disque, le déjeuner du Disque d'Or, organisé par le Variety Club de Grande-Bretagne à l'hôtel Dorchester.

**FRIDAY, MAY 12, 1967**
Recorded in just 16 days and produced by Chandler, the band's debut album, **Are You Experienced** is released in Britain. Showcasing Hendrix's trailblazing guitar chops and imaginative feedback and distortion techniques, it will hit No. 2 in the United Kingdom during a 33-week chart stay, held off the top by the Beatles' **Sgt. Pepper's Lonely Hearts Club Band**.

Das in nur 16 Tagen aufgenommene und von Chas Chandler produzierte Debütalbum der Band, **Are You Experienced** kommt in England auf den Markt. Es demonstriert Jimi Hendrixs bahnbrechende Gitarrentechnik und seinen fantasievollen Einsatz von Feedback und Verzerrung, hält sich 33 Wochen lang in den britischen Charts und schafft es bis auf den 2. Platz – nur **Sgt. Pepper's Lonely Hearts Club Band** von den Beatles hält es vom ersten Platz fern.

Enregistré en seulement 16 jours et produit par Chandler, le premier album du groupe, **Are You Experienced** sort en Grande-Bretagne. Démonstration des tirades avant-gardistes de Hendrix à la guitare et de sa technique maîtrisée de la distorsion et du larsen, il passera 33 semaines dans le classement des meilleures ventes britanniques jusqu'à atteindre la deuxième place, juste derrière le **Sgt. Pepper's Lonely Hearts Club Band** des Beatles.

*"The disk itself is a serious nightmare show, with genuine lust and misery; and also a highly successful blending of simple folk-blues forms with advanced electronic sound effects."*

*„Die Scheibe selbst ist eine Alptraum-Show, voll wahrer Lust und echtem Elend, und außerdem eine extrem erfolgreiche Mischung einfacher Folk-Blues-Formen mit hochmodernen elektronischen Klangeffekten."*

*« Le disque lui-même est un spectacle digne du meilleur cauchemar, empreint d'une luxure et d'une douleur authentiques, qui mélange aussi avec succès les formes simples du folk blues et les effets sonores électriques les plus novateurs. »*

**NEW YORK TIMES**

*"Before I go on stage my road manager says to me: 'Jimi, you scruffy looking git, you're not going on looking like that tonight are you?' And I say: 'As soon as I've put out this cigarette I'm fully dressed.' This is how I like it. I feel comfortable like this."*

*„Bevor ich auf die Bühne gehe, sagt mein Tourmanager zu mir: ‚Jimi, du siehst aus wie ein verlotterter Penner, du willst ja wohl nicht so auf die Bühne gehen?' Und ich sage: ‚Ich brauche nur meine Kippe auszumachen, und schon bin ich fertig.' Solche Klamotten gefallen mir eben. Ich fühle mich wohl so."*

*« Avant que j'entre en scène, mon road-manager me dit : "Jimi, espèce de sale gosse débraillé, tu ne vas pas rester comme ça ce soir, quand même ?"; à quoi je réponds : "Je prends cette cigarette – et je suis habillé." C'est comme ça que ça me plaît. Je me sens bien comme ça. »*

**JIMI HENDRIX, NEW MUSICAL EXPRESS, MAY 13, 1967**

---

**MONDAY, MAY 15, 1967**

The Jimi Hendrix Experience embarks on its first European tour at the Neue Welt in Berlin, West Germany, set to close at the Jaguar Club in Scala, Herford, West Germany, on May 28, following shows in Sweden, Denmark and Finland.

Die Jimi Hendrix Experience spielen zum Auftakt ihrer ersten Europa-Tournee in der Neuen Welt in West-Berlin, der letzte Auftritt findet am 28. Mai nach Konzerten in Schweden, Dänemark und Finnland im Jaguar-Club der Scala in Herford statt.

Le Jimi Hendrix Experience entame au Neue Welt de Berlin-Ouest sa première tournée européenne, qui doit s'achever le 28 mai au Jaguar Club de Scala, à Herford, en Allemagne de l'Ouest, après être passée en Suède, au Danemark et en Finlande.

**MONDAY, MAY 29, 1967**

The Experience tops the bill of "Barbecue '67" at the Tulip Bulb Auction Hall in Spalding, Lincolnshire, also featuring Cream, Geno Washington & the Ram Jam Band, the Move, Pink Floyd and Zoot Money. Admission for the eight-hour concert is £1, with hot dogs, UV soft lights and discotheque provided.

Die Experience spielen als Hauptband beim „Barbecue '67" in der Tulip Bulb Auction Hall in Spalding, Lincolnshire, wo außerdem Cream, Geno Washington & The Ram Jam Band, The Move, Pink Floyd und Zoot Money auftreten. Die Karten für das achtstündige Konzert, bei dem es Hot Dogs, ultraviolettes Schummerlicht und eine Diskothek gibt, kosten ein Pfund.

L'Experience figure en tête d'affiche du festival « Barbecue '67 » au Tulip Bulb Auction Hall de Spalding, dans le Lincolnshire, où se produisent aussi Cream, Geno Washington & the Ram Jam Band, the Move, Pink Floyd et Zoot Money. Pour 1 livre sterling les spectateurs assistent à huit heures de concert, avec distribution de hot-dogs, éclairage feutré et discothèque.

**SUNDAY, JUNE 4, 1967**

With the psychedelic blues rock-fused *The Wind Cries Mary* peaking at No. 6 in the United Kingdom—the group's third successive Top 10 hit—the band performs at the Saville Theatre, on a bill with Procol Harum, the Chiffons and Denny Laine's Electric String Band. With Paul McCartney and George Harrison in attendance, they open with a cover of *Sgt. Pepper's Lonely Hearts Club Band*—only three days since the Beatles album was released.

Während das psychedelische Blues-Stück *The Wind Cries Mary* den 6. Platz in den englischen Charts erreicht – der dritte Top-Ten-Hit in Folge für die Band –, treten sie im Saville Theatre zusammen mit Procol Harum, den Chiffons und Denny Laine's Electric String Band auf. Als sie Paul McCartney und George Harri-son im Publikum sehen, spielen sie als Erstes eine Coverversion von *Sgt. Pepper's Lonely Hearts Club Band* – ganze drei Tage, nachdem das Beatles-Album herausgekommen ist.

Alors que *The Wind Cries Mary*, titre psychédélique imbibé de rock aux tonalités blues, vient d'atteindre la sixième place des meilleures ventes au Royaume-Uni – sa troisième entrée successive dans le Top 10 - le groupe se produit au Saville Theatre, avec Procol Harum, les Chiffons et Denny Laine's Electric String Band. Paul McCartney et George Harrison sont dans la salle, et le groupe commence son set par une reprise de *Sgt. Pepper's Lonely Hearts Club Band* - seulement trois jours après la sortie de l'album des Beatles.

"Bits of the guitar were thrown into the audience for collectors, while Mitch's drum stand was left in a state of collapse. Own up lads, who needs all that?"

„Den Sammlern im Publikum wurden die Bruchstücke der Gitarre vor die Füße geworfen, während Mitchs Schlagzeug als Trümmerhaufen stehen blieb. Nun seid mal ehrlich, Leute: Ist das wirklich notwendig?"

« Des morceaux de la guitare ont été lancés dans le public pour les amateurs de reliques, tandis que la tribune qui avait soutenu la batterie de Mitch était désossée. Non mais franchement les gars, qui a besoin de ces trucs ? »

**CHRIS WELCH, MELODY MAKER, JUNE 10, 1967**

*"In America people are much more narrow-minded than they are in Britain. If they do like us—great! If not—too bad!"*

„*In Amerika sind die Leute wesentlich engstirniger als in England. Wenn sie uns da mögen - wunderbar! Wenn nicht - Pech gehabt!*"

« *En Amérique, les gens sont beaucoup plus bornés qu'en Grande-Bretagne. S'ils nous aiment, tant mieux! Sinon, tant pis!* »

**JIMI HENDRIX, NEW MUSICAL EXPRESS, JUNE 5, 1967**

## SUNDAY, JUNE 18, 1967

In a landmark performance, the Jimi Hendrix Experience makes its United States debut on the final evening of the "Monterey International Pop Festival" at the County Fairgrounds, Monterey, California, having been booked at the urging of Paul McCartney. They only play four original songs, but Hendrix's versions of *Wild Thing* and *Like A Rolling Stone* get a tumultuous reception, especially when he sets fire to, and smashes, his guitar for a familiar finale. (A coin toss won by Pete Townshend has them going on after the Who.)

The Jimi Hendrix Experience spielen zum ersten Mal in den USA und legen am Abschlussabend des „Monterey International Pop Festival" in den County Fairgrounds von Monterey, Kalifornien, einen legendären Auftritt hin. Sie wurden auf Drängen von Paul McCartney gebucht und spielen nur vier eigene Songs, verursachen aber einen größeren Tumult mit *Wild Thing* und *Like A Rolling Stone*, besonders als Jimi Hendrix zum krönenden Abschluss seine Gitarre in Brand steckt und in Stücke haut. (Pete Townshend hatte beim Werfen einer Münze gewonnen und The Experience traten nach The Who auf.)

Au cours d'un concert qui fera date, le Jimi Hendrix Experience fait ses débuts aux États-Unis le dernier soir du festival pop de Monterey (Californie). Le groupe a été engagé à la demande insistante de Paul McCartney. Il ne joue que quatre chansons originales, mais *Wild Thing* et *Like A Rolling Stone* reçoivent un accueil délirant, en particulier quand Hendrix met le feu à sa guitare et la brise en mille morceaux, final grandiose qui fait déjà sa marque. (Hendrix et Pete Townshend ont joué leur ordre de passage à pile ou face, et ce sont les Who qui l'ont emporté.)

The Whisky-A-Go-Go Name Is A Registered Trademark & Is Used By Permission Of W.A.G.G. Inc. • Poster Design & Illustration © 1999 By Dennis Loren • Published By Electric Posters

## MONDAY, JULY 3, 1967 & TUESDAY, JULY 4, 1967

In an unlikely booking, the Experience performs at The Scene in New York, on a bill with the Seeds and Tiny Tim. On Wednesday they will play before a crowd of 18,000 at the Rheingold Festival in Central Park with the Young Rascals. During their time in the city, they stay at the Loew's Motor Inn on 8th Avenue after another hotel refuses to accommodate them.

In einem seltsam zusammengestellten Programm spielen The Experience in The Scene in New York mit The Seeds und Tiny Tim. Am folgenden Mittwoch treten sie vor 18.000 Zuschauern mit den Young Rascals

beim Rheingold Festival im Central Park auf. Sie wohnen in New York im Loew's Motor Inn an der 8th Avenue, nachdem ein anderes Hotel sie abgewiesen hat.

Un curieux attelage se produit au club new-yorkais The Scene, puisque l'Experience partage l'affiche avec les Seeds et Tiny Tim. Le mercredi, ils joueront devant une foule de 18 000 personnes au festival Rheingold, dans Central Park, avec les Young Rascals. Ils logent au Loew's Motor Inn, sur la 8e Avenue, après qu'un autre hôtel a refusé de les accueillir.

*"Enhancing the physical presentation is Hendrix's colorful, bejeweled attire, which combines the aura of Jerry Lee Lewis with that of Liberace."*

*„Jimi Hendrixs körperliche Erscheinung wird noch durch seine farbenfrohe, schmuckbehängte Kleidung verstärkt, in der sich die Aura von Jerry Lee Lewis und Liberace paaren."*

*« L'apparence physique est rendue plus puissante encore par l'allure colorée de Hendrix, paré de bijoux, qui combine l'aura de Jerry Lee Lewis et celle de Liberace. »*

**VARIETY, JULY 12, 1967**

*"Oh God, I hate them! Dishwater. I really hate somebody like that to make it so big. You can't knock anybody for making it, but people like the Monkees?"*

*„Oh Gott, ich hasse sie! Sterbenslangweilig. Ich finde es wirklich schrecklich, wenn solche Leute so berühmt werden. Man kann es ja niemandem übelnehmen, dass er Erfolg hat, aber die Monkees? Nein."*

*« Oh mon Dieu, je les déteste ! C'est du bidon. Je déteste vraiment les gens comme ça qui s'en sortent si bien. On ne peut pas en vouloir aux gens de réussir, mais les Monkees ? »*

**JIMI HENDRIX, MELODY MAKER, JANUARY 28, 1967**

## SATURDAY, JULY 8, 1967

A United States tour with the Monkees opens at the Jacksonville Coliseum in Jacksonville, Florida. As in Britain, Hendrix quickly gains notoriety through the media. The group's music and Hendrix's outrageous often pseudo-erotic showmanship prove inappropriate for the Monkees' teenybop audience and they are dropped after only eight gigs. (Chandler claims that protests from the right-wing Daughters of the American Revolution have brought this about. In reality, however, he knew that the Jeffery-planned support spot would cause welcome controversy and publicity.)

Eine US-Tournee mit den Monkees geht im Jacksonville Coliseum in Jacksonville, Florida, los. Wie in England ist Jimi Hendrix auch hier in den Medien schnell berühmt-berüchtigt. Seine Musik und seine wüste, erotische Bühnenshow erweisen sich als nicht geeignet für das Teeny-Publikum der Monkees und sie werden nach nur acht Gigs herausgeschmissen. (Chas

Chandler behauptet, Proteste der ultrakonservativen Daughters of the American Revolution hätten dazu geführt. In Wirklichkeit wusste er jedoch ganz genau, dass dieser von Mike Jeffery eingefädelte Gig jede Menge erwünschte Kontroversen und Medienrummel verursachen würde.)

La tournée américaine du groupe avec les Monkees est lancée au Coliseum de Jacksonville, en Floride. Comme en Grande-Bretagne, Hendrix se fait rapidement connaître grâce à la presse. La musique du groupe et le jeu scénique sulfureux de Hendrix se révèlent peu compatibles avec la pop édulcorée pour adolescents des Monkees, le public est dérouté et le trio est viré après seulement huit concerts – à cause, d'après Chandler, des protestations des très conservatrices Filles de la Révolution américaine. (En réalité, il savait parfaitement que cette association planifiée par Jeffery provoquerait une polémique et une publicité bienvenues.)

*"Some parents who brought their young kids complained that our act was vulgar. We decided it was just the wrong audience. I think they're replacing me with Mickey Mouse."*

*„Irgendwelche Eltern, die mit ihren Kindern gekommen sind, haben sich beschwert, unsere Show sei vulgär. Da haben wir beschlossen, dass das einfach das falsche Publikum für uns ist. Ich glaube, ich werde durch Micky Maus ersetzt."*

*« Certains parents qui avaient amené leurs enfants se sont plaints parce qu'ils nous trouvaient vulgaires. Nous nous sommes dit que ce public n'était pas fait pour nous. Je crois qu'ils ont pris Mickey à ma place. »*

**JIMI HENDRIX, NEW MUSICAL EXPRESS JULY 29, 1967**

# The "MONKEE'S"

## ★ ★ IN CONCERT ★ ★

## ★ ★ ★ SPECIAL GUEST ★ ★ ★

# JIMI HENDRIX EXPERIENCE

# JULY 8 - 1967 ★ 8:00 P. M.

# JACKSONVILLE COLISEUM

# JACKSONVILLE, FLORIDA

## ★ ★ OPENING CONCERT ★ ★

# U. S. SUMMER TOUR

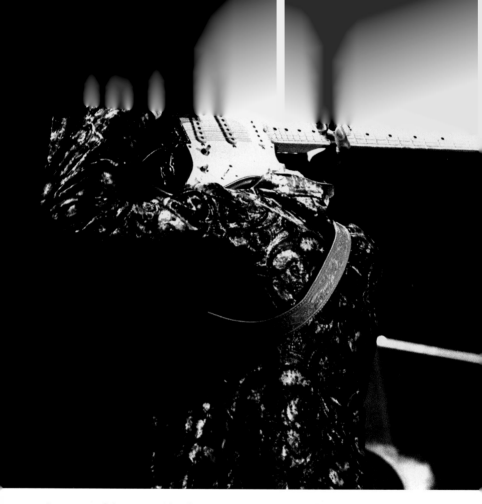

"I wrote part of the song on a plane between LA and New York and finished it in the studios in America. There are some very personal things in there. But I think everyone can understand the feeling when you're traveling that no matter what your address there is no place you can call home. The feeling of man in a little old house in the middle of a desert where he is burning the midnight lamp!"

„Den Song habe ich zum Teil im Flieger von L.A. nach New York geschrieben und in Amerika im Studio fertiggestellt. Er enthält sehr persönliche Dinge. Aber ich glaube, jeder kann das Gefühl verstehen, dass man nirgendwo zu Hause ist, wenn man auf Reisen ist, egal was für eine Adresse man hat. Das ist das Gefühl des Menschen in einem kleinen alten Haus in der Mitte der Wüste, wo er die Mitternachtslampe brennen lässt!"

« J'ai en partie écrit la chanson dans l'avion entre L.A. et New York et je l'ai finie en studio, en Amérique. Elle contient des choses très personnelles. Tout le monde peut comprendre cette impression, quand tu voyages beaucoup et que, où que tu résides, tu ne te sens chez toi nulle part. L'impression que ressent cet homme au fond de sa vieille bicoque, au milieu du désert, quand il fait brûler la lampe de minuit! »

**JIMI HENDRIX, NEW MUSICAL EXPRESS, SEPTEMBER 9, 1967**

## THURSDAY, JULY 20, 1967

Following a gig at the Salvation Club in New York, the Experience finishes recording *Burning Of The Midnight Lamp* at the Mayfair Recording Studio in New York after sessions totalling 42 hours, with Hendrix on harpsichord and Aretha Franklin's backing group, the Sweet Inspirations, on backing vocals.

Nach einem Gig im Salvation Club in New York beenden The Experience im Mayfair Recording Studio in New York die Aufnahmen zu *Burning Of The Midnight Lamp*. Die Sessions dauern insgesamt 42 Stunden, mit Jimi Hendrix am Cembalo und Aretha Franklins Backgroundsängerinnen, den Sweet Inspirations.

Après un concert au Salvation Club de New York, l'Experience file aux studios Mayfair terminer l'enregistrement de *Burning Of The Midnight Lamp* (pour lequel il a déjà 42 heures de son), avec Hendrix au clavecin et le groupe d'Aretha Franklin, les Sweet Inspirations, aux chœurs.

## FRIDAY, AUGUST 18, 1967

Two months after the group's euphoric debut at Monterey, the Experience has a less-than stellar reception at the Hollywood Bowl, supporting the Mamas & the Papas and Scott McKenzie.

Zwei Monate nach dem euphorischen Debüt der Band in Monterey wird ihr in der Hollywood Bowl, wo sie als Vorgruppe von The Mamas & The Papas und Scott McKenzie spielt, ein alles andere als rauschender Empfang bereitet.

Deux mois après les débuts triomphaux du groupe à Monterey, l'Experience reçoit un accueil chaleureux au Hollywood Bowl, en première partie de The Mamas & the Papas et de Scott McKenzie.

*"Jimi Hendrix is a great big hoax. If he can get away with it, then good luck to him. I saw him in Los Angeles. I think he's unexciting and he doesn't move me. The fact that he isn't a big success with the general public proves something."*

*„Jimi Hendrix ist doch ein Riesenschwindel. Wenn ihm das jemand abnimmt, bitte, von mir aus. Aber ich habe ihn in Los Angeles gesehen. Ich finde ihn langweilig und er bewegt mich nicht. Die Tatsache, dass er beim allgemeinen Publikum keinen großen Erfolg genießt, sagt doch alles."*

*« Jimi Hendrix n'est qu'une gigantesque farce. Si les gens mordent à l'hameçon, alors je lui souhaite bonne chance. Je l'ai vu à Los Angeles. Je ne le trouve pas du tout excitant et il ne me touche pas. Le fait qu'il ne soit pas apprécié du grand public prouve bien quelque chose. »*

**PETULA CLARK**

### SUNDAY, AUGUST 27, 1967

Having returned from the United States last weekend, the band makes its fourth appearance at the Saville Theatre in London, with the Crazy World of Arthur Brown and Tomorrow also on the bill. The econd show is canceled after hearing news of the death of the Beatles' manager, Brian Epstein.

The Experience sind am Wochenende zuvor aus den Staaten zurückgekehrt und spielen nun zum vierten Mal im Saville Theatre in London; mit auf der Bühne stehen The Crazy World of Arthur Brown und Tomorrow. Das zweite Konzert wird abgesagt, als der Tod des Beatles-Managers Brian Epstein bekannt wird.

De retour des États-Unis le week-end précédent, le groupe se produit pour la quatrième fois au Saville Theatre de Londres, avec The Crazy World of Arthur Brown et Tomorrow. Le deuxième concert est annulé lorsqu'ils apprennent la mort du manager des Beatles, Brian Epstein.

### THURSDAY, SEPTEMBER 21, 1967

With *Burning Of The Midnight Lamp* currently in the Top 20, Hendrix receives the award for World's Best Pop Musician from **Melody Maker** at its awards ceremony at London's Europa Hotel.

*Burning Of The Midnight Lamp* ist in den Top Twenty und Jimi Hendrix erhält bei einer Feier im Londoner Europa Hotel den Preis als „Bester Popmusiker der Welt" vom **Melody Maker**.

*Burning Of The Midnight Lamp* figure toujours dans les 20 meilleures ventes de disques et Hendrix est sacré Meilleur artiste pop par le magazine **Melody Maker**, à l'Europa Hotel de Londres.

**MONDAY, SEPTEMBER 25, 1967**

The Experience performs at "Guitar-In," a concert at London's Royal Festival Hall, in aid of the Liberal Party, with Bert Jansch, Paco Pena and Sebastian Jorgensen & Tim Walker. Backstage, Hendrix indulges in some hijinx with the Liberal Party leader Jeremy Thorpe.

The Experience spielen beim „Guitar-In", einem Benefiz-Konzert in der Londoner Royal Festival Hall für die britische Liberal Party, mit Bert Jansch, Paco Pena und Sebastian Jorgensen & Tim Walker. Jimi Hendrix albert hinter der Bühne mit dem Vorsitzenden der Liberal Party Jeremy Thorpe herum.

L'Experience participe au « Guitar-In », un concert de soutien au Parti libéral qui se tient au Royal Festival Hall de Londres, avec Bert Jansch, Paco Pena et Sebastian Jorgensen & Tim Walker. En coulisse, Hendrix fait la connaissance du chef du parti, Jeremy Thorpe.

*"Amaze your ears, boggle your mind, flip your lid, do what you want but please get into Hendrix like you never have before—it's just too much."*

*„Bringt euren Kopf um den Verstand, verblüfft eure Ohren, knallt durch, tut, was ihr wollt, aber bitte: Hört Hendrix wie nie zuvor - der Mann ist der totale Wahnsinn."*

*« Ahurissez vos oreilles, bouleversez votre esprit, faites sauter le couvercle, faites comme vous voulez mais je vous en prie, entrez dans l'univers d'Hendrix comme jamais auparavant - c'est simplement trop. »*

**NICK JONES, MELODY MAKER, DECEMBER 9, 1967**

### WEDNESDAY, OCTOBER 25, 1967

The group begins recording at Regent Sound Studios in London for their second album, *Axis: Bold As Love* with Hendrix's "effects man," Roger Mayer, introducing a new Uni-vibe pedal to the sessions which will become another trademark sound for the guitarist.

Die Band beginnt in den Regent Sound Studios in London mit den Plattenaufnahmen für ihr zweites Album *Axis: Bold As Love*. Jimi Hendrixs „Mann für Effekte" Roger Mayer bringt ihm ein neues Univibe Pedal mit, das sich zu einem weiteren Markenzeichen des Gitarristen entwickelt.

Le groupe commence l'enregistrement de son deuxième album, *Axis: Bold As Love*, aux studios Regent Sound de Londres. Le « Monsieur effets spéciaux » de Hendrix, Roger Mayer, apporte au studio sa nouvelle pédale fuzz, qui deviendra une autre marque de fabrique du son Hendrix.

**TUESDAY, NOVEMBER 14, 1967**
The group begins a 15-date, twice-nightly British package tour, with the Move, Pink Floyd, Amen Corner, the Nice and others, at the Royal Albert Hall, set to end December 5 at Green's Playhouse, Glasgow, Scotland. (The Experience will have played almost 200 dates since forming a year ago.)

Die Band geht zusammen mit Move, Pink Floyd, Amen Corner, The Nice und anderen auf eine England-Tournee mit 15 Terminen; das erste Konzert findet in der Royal Albert Hall statt, das letzte am 5. Dezember im Green's Playhouse in Glasgow, Schottland. (Seit Gründung von The Experience vor einem Jahr haben sie fast 200 Auftritte absolviert.)

Le groupe inaugure au Royal Albert Hall une tournée britannique de 15 dates avec, entre autres, The Move, Pink Floyd, Amen Corner ou Nice. Elle s'achèvera le 5 décembre au Green's Playhouse de Glasgow, en Écosse. (Formé une petite année plus tôt seulement, l'Experience a près de 200 concerts à son actif.)

*"I'd like to take a six-month break and go to a school of music. I'm tired of trying to write stuff and finding I can't. I want to write mythology stories set to music, based on a planetary thing and my imagination in general. It wouldn't be similar to classical music but I'd use strings and harps, with extreme and opposite musical textures."*

*„Ich würde gern ein halbes Jahr Pause machen und an einer Musikschule studieren. Ich bin es so leid, Sachen schreiben zu wollen und zu merken, dass ich es nicht kann. Ich möchte mythologische Geschichten schreiben und Musik dazu komponieren, die sich um unseren Planeten dreht und auf meiner Fantasie basiert. Es wäre keine klassische Musik, aber ich würde Saiteninstrumente und Harfen benutzen, mit extremen und widersprüchlichen musikalischen Strukturen."*

*« J'aimerais faire une pause pendant six mois pour aller suivre des cours dans une école de musique. Je suis fatigué d'essayer d'écrire des trucs et de me rendre compte que je n'y arrive pas. Je veux écrire des histoires mythologiques en musique, fondées sur quelque chose de planétaire et sur mon imagination. Ce ne serait pas comme de la musique classique, mais j'utiliserais des cordes et des harpes, avec des textures sonores extrêmes et opposées. »*

**JIMI HENDRIX, MELODY MAKER, DECEMBER 23, 1967**

**FRIDAY, DECEMBER 22, 1967**
The trio participates in the "Christmas On Earth Continued" concert at London's Olympia, with the Who, the Move, Traffic, Eric Burdon & the Animals and Pink Floyd, among others.

Das Trio nimmt an dem Konzert „Christmas On Earth Continued" im Londoner Olympia teil. Es spielen The Who, The Move, Traffic, Eric Burdon & The Animals, Pink Floyd u.a.

Le trio participe au concert « Christmas On Earth Continued » à l'Olympia de Londres, avec les Who, les Move, Traffic, Eric Burdon & the Animals et Pink Floyd, entre autres.

© Christie's

*"I'm just a frustrated old hen. That's all. That's what I feel like ... I really don't give a damn about my future or my career. I just want to make sure I can get out what I want."*

*„Ich bin eine frustrierte alte Glucke. Sonst nichts. Genau so fühle ich mich – meine Zukunft oder meine Karriere sind mir scheißegal, wirklich. Ich will nur das ausdrücken, was in mir ist."*

*« Je ne suis qu'un vieux coq frustré. C'est tout. C'est comme ça que je me sens... Je me fous complètement de mon avenir et de ma carrière. Je veux juste être sûr de pouvoir sortir ce que je veux. »*

**JIMI HENDRIX, DECEMBER 1967**

# 1968

*"... the Wilt Chamberlain of electric guitar players.
If Wilt can make a basketball look like something he picked off an orange tree,
Jimi can make a guitar look like something he uses to pick his teeth."*

*„... der Wilt Chamberlain der elektrischen Gitarre.
Bei Wilt sieht ein Basketball aus wie etwas, das er gerade
vom nächsten Orangenbaum gepflückt hat, und bei Jimi hat man den Eindruck,
die Gitarre wäre etwas, womit er sich in den Zähnen stochert."*

*« [...] Le Wilt Chamberlain des joueurs de guitare électrique.
Si entre les mains de Wilt un ballon de basket peut avoir l'air d'avoir été cueilli
sur un oranger, Jimi sait faire ressembler une guitare à un cure-dents. »*

**ALFRED G. ARONOWITZ, LIFE, MARCH 15, 1968**

## THURSDAY, JANUARY 4, 1968

The group begins a four-date Scandinavian tour at the Lorensberg Cirkus in Gothenburg, Sweden, promoting *Axis: Bold As Love*. Tensions are developing, both within the group and with management. Hendrix is incarcerated overnight in a Swedish jail, after wrecking his room at the Hotel Opalen. He will be fined 8,918 krones—and have to be escorted to the concert by police, his right hand in bandages.

Die Band geht mit *Axis: Bold As Love* auf Skandinavien-Tournee und spielt den ersten von vier Gigs im Lorensberg Cirkus in Göteborg. Die Spannungen innerhalb der Gruppe und mit dem Management wachsen. Jimi Hendrix muss die Nacht in einem schwedischen Gefängnis verbringen, nachdem er sein Zimmer im Hotel Opalen zertrümmert hat. Er erhält eine Geldstrafe in Höhe von 8.918 Kronen – und wird mit verbundener rechter Hand von der Polizei zum Konzert gebracht.

Le groupe commence une tournée scandinave de quatre dates au Lorensberg Cirkus de Gothenburg, en Suède, pour la promotion d'*Axis: Bold As Love*. Les tensions s'intensifient, à la fois au sein du groupe et avec les organisateurs. Hendrix passe la nuit en prison pour avoir vandalisé sa chambre de l'hôtel Opalen. Il devra payer une amende de 8 918 couronnes et sera escorté au concert par la police, la main droite bandée.

**WEDNESDAY, JANUARY 31, 1968**
Hendrix attends "The British Are Coming" press reception at the Copter Club in the Pan Am Building in New York.

Jimi Hendrix nimmt am Presseempfang „The British Are Coming" im Copter Club im Pan Am Building in New York teil.

Hendrix assiste à la conférence de presse « The British Are Coming », organisée au Copter Club, dans l'immeuble de la Pan Am, à New York.

100

© Christie's

### THURSDAY, FEBRUARY 1, 1968

The Experience begins a three-month American tour at the Fillmore West in San Francisco. The group reportedly earns a guaranteed $500,000 plus a percentage of the profits. Still courting controversy, the Dean of Boston College bans the group from appearing at the school on March 28.

The Experience starten im Fillmore West in San Francisco eine dreimonatige Amerika-Tournee, mit der sie angeblich eine halbe Million Dollar garantiert plus Gewinnbeteiligung verdienen. Die Gruppe sorgt nach wie vor für Kontroversen, der Rektor des Boston College verbietet ihren Auftritt im College am 28. März.

L'Experience commence sa tournée américaine de trois mois au Fillmore West de San Francisco. Le groupe aurait touché un cachet de 500 000 dollars assorti d'un pourcentage sur les bénéfices. La polémique lui colle à la peau et le doyen de l'université de Boston interdit que le groupe se produise sur son campus le 28 mars.

JIMI HENDRIX
EXPERIENCE
JOHN MAYALL
AND THE BLUESBREAKERS

ALBERT KING

FEB 1–4 THUR-SUN
FILLMORE
LIGHTS BY HOLY SEE

4

FEB 2–3 FRI-SAT
WINTERLAND
LIGHTS BY JERRY ABRAMS HEAD LIGHTS

TICKETS

**MONDAY, FEBRUARY 12, 1968**
  With his home country finally discovering his music (his debut album, **Are You Experienced**, about to make the Top 10), Hendrix performs a hometown gig in Seattle, Washington at the Center Arena. The next day he returns to Garfield High School, which he attended as a boy, but with too little sleep and the early morning hour, his appearance is muted and met with indifference.

  Jimi Hendrixs Heimatland entdeckt endlich seine Musik (sein Debüt-Album **Are You Experienced** steht kurz vor dem Eintritt in die Top Ten) und er spielt in seiner Heimatstadt Seattle, Washington, in der Center Arena. Am nächsten Tag besucht er die Garfield High School, wo er in die Schule gegangen ist, aber es ist zu früh am Morgen und er ist unausgeschlafen, sein Auftreten ist wenig überzeugend und stößt auf Gleichgültigkeit.

  Alors que son pays natal découvre enfin sa musique (son premier album, **Are You Experienced**, frôle alors le Top 10), Hendrix joue à domicile, au Center Arena de Seattle. Le lendemain, il va visiter le lycée Garfield, qu'il a fréquenté adolescent, mais il a peu dormi, il est très tôt, et son apparition passe quasiment inaperçue.

### SUNDAY, FEBRUARY 25, 1968

As **Axis: Bold As Love** peaks at No. 3 in the United States, during a year-long chart stay, Hendrix is interviewed in the **New York Times**. Commenting on music, the army, Bob Dylan and life, he says: "Man, it's the music, that's what comes first. People who put down the performance, they're people who can't use their eyes and ears at the same time. They got a button on their shoulder blades that keeps only one working at a time ... Anybody could be in the Army, I had to do it special, but man, was I bored ... Dylan really turned me on – not the words or his guitar, but as a way to get myself together. A cat like that can do it to you ... In this life you gotta go what you want, you gotta let your mind and fancy flow, flow, flow free."

*Axis: Bold As Love* erreicht den dritten Platz in den USA und hält sich ein ganzes Jahr lang in den Charts. Jimi Hendrix wird von der **New York Times** interviewt. Er äußert sich zur Musik, zur Armee, zu Bob Dylan und dem Leben im Allgemeinen: „Die Musik ist es, Mann, die Musik steht an erster Stelle. Die Leute, die schlecht über Live-Auftritte reden, das sind doch Leute, die ihre Augen und Ohren nicht gleichzeitig benutzen können. Die haben einen Knopf an der Schulter, mit dem sie nur eins von beidem einschalten können ... Zur Armee gehen, das kann ja jeder, ich musste mir natürlich was Besonderes heraussuchen, aber ich habe mich so verdammt gelangweilt da ... Dylan macht mich sehr an – nicht die Texte oder wie er Gitarre spielt, sondern als Vorbild, wie man die Kurve kriegen kann. Das kann dir einer wie er klarmachen ... In diesem Leben muss man hinter dem hinterher sein, was man will, du musst deinen Kopf und deine Gefühle frei fließen lassen, ganz frei, frei, frei."

*Axis: Bold As Love* atteint la troisième place des ventes aux États-Unis après plus d'un an de figuration au classement, et Hendrix est interviewé par le New York Times. Il y parle de musique, de l'armée, de Bob Dylan et de la vie en général : « Mec, c'est la musique, c'est ça qui passe d'abord. Les gens qui critiquent la performance scénique, ce sont des gens qui ne savent pas utiliser en même temps leurs yeux et leurs oreilles. Ils ont un interrupteur sur les omoplates qui fait qu'ils se servent de l'un ou de l'autre... Tout le monde peut faire l'armée, j'étais obligé d'y aller, encore plus que les autres, mais mec, qu'est-ce que je me suis ennuyé ! [...] Dylan m'a vraiment excité – pas avec ses mots, ou sa musique, mais il m'a touché. Un type comme ça peut te faire ça. [...] Dans la vie, il faut faire ce dont on a envie, il faut laisser son esprit et son imagination flotter, flotter, libres. »

### WEDNESDAY, MARCH 13, 1968

Record Plant Studios—a partnership between industry veterans Chris Stone, Gary Kellgren, Tom Wilson and Wes Farrell—opens its doors in New York. The studio's first client is Hendrix, whose drawn-out sessions for what will become the **Electric Ladyland** album, will help the fledgling studio build its legendary reputation.

Die Record-Plant-Studios – gegründet von den Branchenveteranen Chris Stone, Gary Kellgren, Tom Wilson und Wes Farrell – öffnen ihre Türen in New York. Erster Kunde des Plattenstudios ist Jimi Hendrix, dessen lang gezogene Aufnahmesessions für das Album **Electric Ladyland** dem Jungstudio zu seinem legendären Ruf verhelfen.

Les Studios Record Plant – un partenariat entre les vétérans de l'industrie du disque Chris Stone, Gary Kellgren, Tom Wilson et Wes Farrell – ouvrent à New York. Hendrix est leur premier client et les séances d'enregistrement laborieuses qui donneront naissance à l'album **Electric Ladyland** l'aideront à acquérir sa réputation légendaire.

**FRIDAY, APRIL 5, 1968**
Hendrix plays an all-night blues session with B. B. King and Buddy Guy at the Generation Club in New York, the night after Martin Luther King's assassination.

Am Abend nach der Ermordung von Martin Luther King spielt Jimi Hendrix eine ganze Nacht lang bei einer Blues-Session mit B. B. King und Buddy Guy im Generation Club in New York.

Le lendemain de l'assassinat de Martin Luther King, Hendrix passe la nuit à jouer du blues avec B. B. King et Buddy Guy au Generation Club de New York.

**THURSDAY, MAY 2, 1968**
Back in the studio having completed his latest live commitments during an unendingly busy schedule, Hendrix records the 15-minute track, *Voodoo Chile* during further **Electric Ladyland** sessions at Record Plant. Increasingly at odds with Redding, Hendrix has brought in Jefferson Airplane bassist Jack Casady and Traffic keyboardist, Steve Winwood (keyboards) for the recording of what will become another seminal career highlight. The double album will be released in September to universal critical praise and worldwide commercial success.

Mit seinem stets übervollen Terminkalender hat Jimi Hendrix die aktuellen Live-Verpflichtungen hinter sich gebracht und kehrt ins Record-Plant-Studio zurück, wo er das fünfzehnminütige Stück *Voodoo Chile* für die LP **Electric Ladyland** aufnimmt. Da es immer größere Auseinandersetzungen mit Noel Redding gibt, hat Jimi Hendrix den Bassisten von Jefferson Airplane, Jack Casady, und den Keyboarder von Traffic, Steve Winwood, zu der Session mitgebracht, die zu einem weiteren großen Höhepunkt seiner Karriere wird. Das Doppelalbum kommt im September auf den Markt, wird von der Kritik gefeiert und verkauft sich weltweit hervorragend.

De retour en studio après avoir honoré les derniers engagements de son agenda de concerts, surchargé, Hendrix enregistre un morceau de 15 minutes, *Voodoo Chile*, qu'il intégrera à **Electric Ladyland**. Ses relations avec Redding se dégradent et Hendrix fait appel au bassiste de Jefferson Airplane, Jack Casady, et au clavier de Traffic Steve Winwood pour ces séances qui marquent un nouvel apogée de sa carrière. Le double album sortira en septembre et rencontrera un succès commercial et critique mondial.

*"Sound on sound, they go go go, and where the rockers'll stop, nobody knows—as long as youngsters keep shelling out top coin for fourth class showmanship."*

*„Hier ein Klang, da ein Klang, immer weiter, weiter, weiter, und ob die Rocker vor irgendwas zurückschrecken werden, weiß man nicht – nicht solange die Kids harte Münze für viertklassige Shows springen lassen."*

*« Son après son, ils avancent, avancent, avancent, et personne ne peut dire où ces rockeurs s'arrêteront – tant que les jeunes continueront à dépenser leur argent de poche pour un spectacle de quatrième classe. »*

**VARIETY, MARCH 6, 1968**

### THURSDAY, MAY 30 & FRIDAY, MAY 31, 1968

Following three dates in Italy, the Experience takes part in two "Monster-Konzerts" at the Hallenstadion, Zurich, Switzerland, with Eric Burdon & the Animals, John Mayall's Bluesbreakers, the Move, the Small Faces, Traffic and others. At the Friday soundcheck, Hendrix, Stevie Winwood, Chris Wood, Trevor Burton, Carl Wayne and Vic Briggs jam together.

Nach drei Auftritten in Italien nehmen The Experience an zwei „Monster-Konzerten" im Hallenstadion in Zürich teil, zusammen mit Eric Burdon & The Animals, John Mayall's Bluesbreakers, The Move, The Small Faces, Traffic und anderen. Beim Soundcheck am Freitag jammen Jimi Hendrix, Stevie Winwood, Chris Wood, Trevor Burton, Carl Wayne und Vic Briggs zusammen.

Après trois dates en Italie, l'Experience participe à deux « Monster-Konzerts » au Hallenstadion de Zurich, en Suisse, avec Eric Burdon & the Animals, John Mayall's Bluesbreakers, The Move, les Small Faces et Traffic, entre autres. La répétition du vendredi tourne au bœuf entre Hendrix, Stevie Winwood, Chris Wood, Trevor Burton, Carl Wayne et Vic Briggs.

"It was noted that Jimi Hendrix played the guitar with his teeth, his elbow, his head and even his hindquarters. It is also rumoured that at one stage his hands came into contact with the strings."

„Wie man feststellen konnte, spielte Jimi Hendrix die Gitarre mit den Zähnen, dem Ellbogen, seinem Kopf und sogar dem Hinterteil. Wenn man Gerüchten Glauben schenken will, kamen irgendwann sogar seine Hände in Kontakt mit den Saiten."

« D'après des témoins, Jimi Hendrix a joué de la guitare avec ses dents, son coude, sa tête, et même son arrière-train. La rumeur veut aussi qu'à un moment, ses mains soient entrées en contact avec les cordes. »

**RICHARD GREEN, NEW MUSICAL EXPRESS, JUNE 8, 1968**

### SATURDAY, JULY 6, 1968

The Experience tops the bill on the first night of the two-day "Woburn Music Festival," at Woburn Abbey— some 40 miles north of London and the home of the Duke of Bedford. An estimated 8,000 people attend the weekend event, despite poor weather on Sunday. Not everyone is happy about the festival: the landlord of the Birchmoor Arms pub will complain to the local **Bedfordshire Times** "They left Woburn looking as though it had been bombed."

The Experience sind die Headliner am ersten Abend des zweitägigen „Woburn Music Festival" in der Woburn Abbey, rund 65 km nördlich von London auf dem Landsitz des Duke of Bedford. Schätzungsweise 8.000 Leute kommen zu dem Open-Air-Event, trotz schlechten Wetters am Sonntag. Nicht alle sind begeistert von dem Festival: Der Besitzer des Birchmoor Arms Pubs klagt der Zeitung **Bedfordshire Times** sein Leid: „Als sie weg waren, sah Woburn aus, als hätte eine Bombe eingeschlagen."

L'Experience occupe la tête d'affiche au premier soir du festival de deux jours de Woburn Abbey – qui se tient sur les terres du duc de Bedford, à une soixantaine de kilomètres au nord de Londres.

Quelque 8 000 personnes y assistent, malgré la météo maussade du dimanche, mais tout le monde ne se réjouit pas de ce succès : le propriétaire du pub Birchmoor Arms se plaint au journal local, le **Bedfordshire Times** : « Ils ont laissé Woburn dans un chaos digne d'un lendemain de bombardement. »

### SATURDAY, JULY 6, 1968

Hendrix settles the suit brought against him by Ed Chalpin, made before Judge Dudley Bonsal in New York Federal Court, a deal which could net Chalpin's P.P.X. Enterprises $1,000,000 over the next three years.

Jimi Hendrix stimmt einer gerichtlichen Einigung mit Ed Chalpin vor Richter Dudley Bonsal am New Yorker Bundesgericht zu. Chalpins P.P.X. Enterprises könnten damit im Laufe der nächsten drei Jahre eine Million Dollar verdienen.

Hendrix règle le conflit qui l'oppose à Ed Chalpin devant la cour fédérale de New York, sous les auspices du juge Dudley Bonsal, par un accord susceptible de rapporter un million de dollars à P.P.X. Enterprises, la compagnie de Chalpin, les trois années suivantes.

*"People were starting to take us for granted, abuse us.
It was that what-cornflakes-for-breakfast scene. Pop slavery really."*

*„Die Leute fingen an, uns als selbstverständlich hinzunehmen
und uns auszunutzen. So nach der Art: Was, Corn Flakes zum Frühstück!
Es war wirklich die absolute Pop-Sklavenhalter-Mentalität."*

*« Les gens se mettaient à nous traiter comme de la m..., à profiter de
nous. De l'esclavagisme pop, en fait. »*

**JIMI HENDRIX, MELODY MAKER**

**MONDAY, JULY 15, 1968**

The Experience performs at the opening of Chandler and Jeffery's Sergeant Peppers club off the Plaza Gomilla in Palma, Majorca. During the set, Hendrix puts the neck of his guitar through the low ceiling. On Tuesday they go to the beach at Lauro Verde where Hendrix ventures into the sea for the first time in eight years. Wednesday they go go-karting, and return to the club in the evening, playing a set which includes *Johnny B. Goode* and *Lucille*.

The Experience spielen bei der Eröffnung von Chas Chandlers und Mike Jefferys Sergeant Peppers Club an der Plaza Gomilla in Palma auf Mallorca. Bei dem Auftritt durchbohrt Hendrix die niedrige Decke mit dem Hals seiner Gitarre. Am Dienstag gehen sie in Lauro Verde an den Strand, wo Jimi Hendrix zum ersten Mal seit acht Jahren im Meer schwimmt. Am Mittwoch fahren sie Gokarts, abends spielen sie noch einen Set im Club, u.a. die Stücke *Johnny B. Goode* und *Lucille*.

L'Experience se produit lors de l'inauguration du Sergeant Peppers, le club ouvert par Chandler et Jeffery sur la Plaza Gomilla de Palma, à Majorque. Pendant leur passage, Hendrix perce le plafond bas de la salle avec la tête de sa guitare. Le lendemain, ils vont à la plage de Lauro Verde, où Hendrix se baigne pour la première fois depuis huit ans. Le mercredi, ils vont faire du karting et reviennent au club le soir pour un nouveau set qui inclut *Johnny B. Goode* et *Lucille*.

**SATURDAY, SEPTEMBER 14, 1968**

On the penultimate date of a 47-date, six-week North American tour, the group makes a more successful return visit to the Hollywood Bowl, with several fans cavorting in the water.

Das vorletzte Konzert einer sechswöchigen Tournee mit 47 Konzerten findet in der Hollywood Bowl statt, wo die Band diesmal wesentlich besser bei den Fans ankommt, die zum Teil im Wasser herumplanschen.

L'avant-dernier soir de sa tournée de six semaines, le groupe fait un retour plus réussi au Hollywood Bowl; plusieurs fans vont s'ébattre dans l'eau.

**THURSDAY, OCTOBER 17, 1968**

With Hendrix's cover version of Bob Dylan's *All Along The Watchtower* reaching its American No. 20 peak this week—and Chas Chandler relinquishing his managerial interest in the band—the group begins rehearsing at TTG Recording Studios in Hollywood.

In dieser Woche erreicht Jimi Hendrixs Coverversion von Bob Dylans *All Along The Watchtower* den amerikanischen Höchststand auf Platz 20 – und Chas Chandler hört als Manager der Band auf, die nun mit Proben in den TTG Recording Studios in Hollywood beginnt.

Hendrix atteint la vingtième place des meilleures ventes en Amérique avec sa reprise du titre de Bob Dylan, *All Along The Watchtower*; Chas Chandler renonce à s'occuper plus longtemps du groupe, qui commence les répétitions dans les studios TTG, à Hollywood.

**WEDNESDAY, NOVEMBER 6, 1968**

Police turn up at trendy Piccadilly Circus boutique I Was Lord Kitchener's Valet in London, after owner John Paul has dressed his front window with three scantily-clad models promoting the new Experience album *Electric Ladyland*. The gathered crowd is warned that they are causing an obstruction and Paul is told that he will be reported.

Die schicke Boutique I Was Lord Kitchener's Valet am Piccadilly Circus in London wird von der Polizei gestürmt, nachdem Besitzer John Paul das Schaufenster mit drei kaum bekleideten Models dekoriert hat,

die für das neue Experience-Album *Electric Ladyland* werben. Die Menschenansammlung auf dem Bürgersteig wird zum Weitergehen aufgefordert und John Paul wird verwarnt.

La police londonienne fait une descente à la boutique branchée « I Was Lord Kitchener's Valet », sur Piccadilly Circus, dont le gérant, John Paul, a disposé dans sa vitrine trois mannequins légèrement vêtus en hommage au nouvel opus de l'Experience, *Electric Ladyland*. La foule présente est menacée d'arrestation pour obstruction et Paul reçoit un avertissement.

"Mitch and Noel want to get their own thing going ... So very soon, probably in the New Year, we'll be breaking the group—apart from selected dates."

„Mitch und Noel wollen ihr eigenes Ding machen ... Wir werden uns also ziemlich bald, wahrscheinlich im neuen Jahr, als Gruppe auflösen - abgesehen von einzelnen Auftritten."

« Mitch et Noel ont envie de tracer leur propre route. [...] Donc très bientôt, sans doute autour du Nouvel An, nous allons dissoudre le groupe - à part pour certains concerts précis. »

**JIMI HENDRIX, MELODY MAKER, NOVEMBER 16, 1968**

**THURSDAY, NOVEMBER 28, 1968**
In the midst of another American tour, the Experience becomes the first rock band to play at New York's Philharmonic Hall in an evening of music titled "An Electronic Thanksgiving."

The Experience sind auf einer erneuten US-Tournee die erste Rockband, die in der Philharmonic Hall in New York spielt. Das Konzert findet unter dem Motto „An Electronic Thanksgiving" statt.

L'Experience, alors encore en pleine tournée américaine, devient le premier groupe de rock à jouer au célèbre Philarmonic Hall de New York, à l'occasion de la soirée « An Electronic Thanksgiving ».

*"It all begins to make sense if we view the superstar, Mr. Hendrix, as a great classical virtuoso. He breaks strings, as did Paganini. He postures as did Liszt. He deals in thunderous climaxes, as did Beethoven."*

*„Wenn wir den Superstar, Mr. Hendrix, als großen klassischen Virtuosen betrachten, ergibt das alles auf einmal einen Sinn. Er bringt die Saiten zum Reißen wie Paganini. Er wirft sich in Posen wie Liszt. Er liebt die donnernden Höhepunkte wie Beethoven."*

*« Tout prend un sens si on considère M. Hendrix la superstar comme un grand virtuose classique. Il casse des cordes, comme Paganini. Il se tient comme Liszt. Il affectionne les montées tonitruantes, comme Beethoven. »*

**ROBERT SHELTON, NEW YORK TIMES, NOVEMBER 29, 1968**

**SUNDAY, DECEMBER 1, 1968**
The four-month North American tour comes to a close at the Coliseum in Chicago. Pressures on Hendrix increase, with the departure of Chandler taking its toll. The group temporarily splits, with Mitchell and Redding returning to Britain without Hendrix. (The day after Christmas, Hendrix will tear several ligaments after falling in heavy snow in New York, which will force the cancellation of an appearance at the Utrecht Pop Festival at the end of the month.)

© Christie's

Die viermonatige Nordamerika-Tournee endet im Coliseum in Chicago. Der Druck auf Jimi Hendrix nimmt zu; das Fehlen von Chas Chandler macht sich negativ bemerkbar. Die Gruppe löst sich vorübergehend auf und Mitch und Noel kehren ohne Jimi nach England zurück. Am zweiten Weihnachtsfeiertag reißt Jimi Hendrix sich mehrere Sehnen, als er im Tiefschnee in New York hinfällt, weswegen ein Auftritt beim Utrecht Pop Festival Ende des Monats abgesagt wird.

La tournée américaine de quatre mois s'achève au Coliseum de Chicago. Hendrix subit une pression croissante, et les conséquences du départ de Chandler se font. Le groupe se sépare temporairement et Mitchell et Redding retournent en Grande-Bretagne sans Hendrix. (Le lendemain de Noël, Hendrix se déchire plusieurs ligaments en tombant sous la neige, à New York, et doit annuler sa participation à l'Utrecht Pop Festival, à la fin du mois.)

# 1969

"For the volatile hard core—the 14-to-19 bag—Jimi is not so much the Experience
as the menace to public health. Plugged in and zonked, he only has to step
across the stage (which he does like a high-strutting chicken going after a kernel of corn)
to turn on their high-pitched passion."

„Für den empfänglichen harten Kern seiner Fans – die 14- bis 19-Jährigen – ist Jimi weniger eine
Erfahrung als vielmehr eine Gefahr für die öffentliche Gesundheit. Er weiß, was abgeht, er ist total
drauf und braucht bloß über die Bühne zu stolzieren (was er tut wie ein aufgeregtes Huhn, das einem
Maiskorn hinterherjagt), und schon schreien die Kids sich vor Inbrunst die Seele aus dem Leib."

« Pour le noyau dur très volatile que constituent les fans de 14 à 19 ans,
Jimi représente, plus qu'une Expérience, une menace à la santé publique.
Branché sur l'électricité, l'air épuisé, il lui suffit de fouler la scène – ce qu'il fait comme un poulet
se pavanant pour un épi de maïs – pour déclencher leur passion hystérique. »

**LOOK, MARCH 18, 1969**

*"We'd like to stop playing this rubbish and dedicate a song to the Cream regardless of what kind of group they might be in. I'd like to dedicate this to Eric Clapton, Ginger Baker and Jack Bruce."*

*„Wir wollen jetzt aufhören, diesen Quatsch zu spielen und lieber Cream einen Song widmen, auch wenn sie jetzt in anderen Gruppen spielen. Das hier ist für Eric Clapton, Ginger Baker und Jack Bruce."*

*« On aimerait arrêter de jouer cette camelote et dédier une chanson aux Cream, quel que soit le groupe dans lequel ils sont. Je voudrais dédier ça à Eric Clapton, Ginger Baker et Jack Bruce. »*

**JIMI HENDRIX**

### SATURDAY, JANUARY 4, 1969

The group performs live on BBC1-TV's "Happening For Lulu." 2 minutes and 34 seconds into a performance of *Hey Joe*, they stop and launch into an impromptu version of *Sunshine Of Your Love*, as a tribute to the recently-split Cream, much to the annoyance of the program's producers. During a break in rehearsals earlier, Hendrix tells **Melody Maker**'s Chris Welch that the group is not splitting up—"The group itself will always be together as long as we are still breathing."

Das Trio ist live im BBC1-Fernsehen bei „Happening For Lulu" zu sehen. Nach 2 Minuten und 34 Sekunden unterbrechen sie *Hey Joe* und schwenken auf eine Spontan-Version von *Sunshine Of Your Love* um, ein Tribut an Cream, die sich gerade aufgelöst haben, sehr zum Ärger der Produzenten der Sendung. Während einer Probenpause erzählt Jimi Hendrix Chris Welch vom **Melody Maker**, dass die Gruppe sich doch nicht auflöst: „Solange wir noch atmen, solange wird auch die Gruppe zusammenbleiben."

Le groupe se réunit pour l'émission culte de la BBC1 « Happening For Lulu ». Après 2 minutes et 34 secondes de *Hey Joe*, il s'interrompt pour enchaîner sur une version impromptue de *Sunshine Of Your Love*, en hommage à Cream, récemment dissout, provoquant l'agacement des producteurs de l'émission. Pendant les répétitions, au cours d'une pause, Hendrix a déclaré au journaliste du **Melody Maker** Chris Welch que l'Experience ne se sépare pas – « Le groupe restera toujours uni, tant qu'on respirera. »

**FRIDAY, FEBRUARY 14, 1969**
Bee Gees Maurice Gibb presents Hendrix with the award for World's Best Musician at **Disc & Music Echo**'s Valentine's Day Awards at London's Seymour Hall.

Maurice Gibb von den Bee Gees überreicht Jimi Hendrix den Preis „Bester Musiker der Welt" bei den Valentine's Day Awards des **Disc & Music Echo**. Die Preisverleihung findet in der Londoner Seymour Hall statt.

Maurice Gibb desBee Gees remet à Hendrix le prix de Meilleur musicien du monde lors de la cérémonie des « Valentine's Day Awards » de **Disc & Music Echo**, au Seymour Hall de Londres.

*"I can't play guitar any more the way I want to. I get very frustrated on stage when we play."*

*„Ich kann nicht mehr so Gitarre spielen, wie ich will. Wenn wir auf der Bühne stehen und spielen, bin ich schrecklich frustriert."*

*« Je ne peux plus jouer de la guitare comme je veux. Je suis très frustré quand nous jouons sur scène. »*

**JIMI HENDRIX, STOCKHOLM RADIO INTERVIEW, JANUARY, 1969**

**TUESDAY, FEBRUARY 18 &
MONDAY, FEBRUARY 24, 1969**

On the verge of breaking up, the Jimi Hendrix Experience plays its last United Kingdom concerts, sold-out affairs at London's Royal Albert Hall. During the finale at the second performance, Traffic's Dave Mason and Chris Wood jam with them on *Room Full Of Mirrors*.

Das Trio steht kurz vor der Trennung und gibt seine letzten Konzerte in England in der völlig ausverkauften Royal Albert Hall. Beim zweiten Auftritt gesellen sich Dave Mason und Chris Wood von Traffic zum Finale mit *Room Full Of Mirrors* auf die Bühne.

Toujours au bord de la rupture, le Jimi Hendrix Experience donne ses derniers concerts britanniques au Royal Albert Hall de Londres. Le deuxième soir, les musiciens de Traffic Dave Mason et Chris Wood le rejoignent sur scène pour le dernier morceau, *Room Full Of Mirrors*.

*"In his field he is a Segovia or Manitas de Plata except that his guitar is electric. A packed house stood and roared their approval at everything he did."*

*„Er ist der Segovia oder Manitas de Plata der elektrischen Gitarre. Alle im überfüllten Saal waren auf den Beinen und taten brüllend ihre Zustimmung zu allem kund, was er tat."*

*« Il est le Segovia ou le Manitas de Plata de la guitare électrique. Dans la salle pleine à craquer, le public, debout, rugissait à chacun de ses gestes. »*

**RICHARD GREEN, NEW MUSICAL EXPRESS,
FEBRUARY 22, 1969**

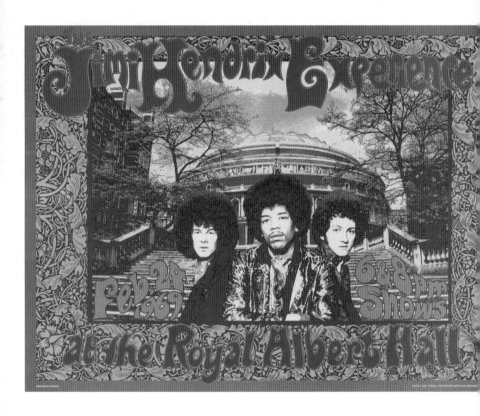

"'It's funny the way most people love the dead. Once you are dead you are made for life. You have to die before they think you are worth anything."

„Es ist schon seltsam, wie die Leute die Toten lieben. Wenn man erst mal tot ist, dann hat man den Durchbruch geschafft. Man muss erst sterben, bevor man etwas zählt."

« C'est étrange comme la plupart des gens aiment les morts. Une fois qu'on est mort, on devient quelqu'un. Il faut qu'on meure pour qu'ils pensent qu'on vaut quelque chose. »

**JIMI HENDRIX IN AN INTERVIEW WITH MELODY MAKER'S BOB DAWBARN, FEBRUARY 25, 1969**

## TUESDAY, MARCH 18, 1969

Already a popular staple during his live sets, Hendrix records the American national anthem, *The Star Spangled Banner* and *Hey Gypsy Boy* at the Record Plant in New York with producer and longtime engineer, Eddie Kramer.

Jimi Hendrix nimmt *The Star Spangled Banner* und *Hey Gypsy Boy* im Record Plant in New York zusammen mit dem Produzenten und langjährigen Toninge-nieur Eddie Kramer auf. Bei Live-Auftritten hat er die amerikanische Nationalhymne schon oft gespielt.

Hendrix enregistre ce qui est déjà le clou de ses performances scéniques, sa version très personnelle de l'hymne américain, *Star Spangled Banner* (la « Bannière étoilée »), ainsi que *Hey Gypsy Boy*, aux studios Record Plant de New York, avec son fidèle ingénieur du son Eddie Kramer à la production.

*"He combines the phantasmagoric splendor of a Hieronymous Bosch painting with the funky essence of rhythm and blues. The cat is out of sight."*

*„Er verbindet die überbordende Fantasie eines Hieronymous-Bosch-Gemäldes mit dem funkigen Herzen des Rhythm and Blues. Der Mann ist der komplette Wahnsinn."*

*« Il cumule la splendeur fantasmagorique d'une toile de Hieronymous Bosch avec l'essence funky du Rhythm and Blues. Ce type est hallucinant. »*

**TOM WILSON, LOOK, MARCH 18, 1969**

"What I want to do is rest completely for one year. Completely. I'll have to. Maybe something'll happen and I'll break my own rules, but I'll have to try. It's the physical and emotional toll I have to think of."

„Ich will ein Jahr lang total Pause machen. Total. Das muss ich. Vielleicht passiert irgendetwas und ich breche meinen guten Vorsatz, aber ich muss es versuchen. Ich muss an die körperlichen und emotionalen Folgen denken."

« Ce que je veux, c'est me reposer complètement pendant un an. Il faut que je le fasse. Peut-être que quelque chose arrivera et que je briserai la règle que je me suis fixée, mais il faut que j'essaie. Il faut que je pense au prix physique et émotionnel que je risque de payer. »

**JIMI HENDRIX, APRIL 1969**

### FRIDAY, APRIL 11, 1969

A 23-date North American tour begins at the J.S. Dorton Arena in Raleigh, North Carolina—with Noel Redding's new band, Fat Mattress, as support. The tour will end with the last of three consecutive shows at the Waikiki Shell in Honolulu, Hawaii on June 1.

Auftakt zu einer Nordamerikatournee mit 23 Konzerten in der J.S. Dorton Arena in Raleigh, North Carolina mit Noel Reddings neuer Band Fat Mattress.

Die Tour endet mit drei Auftritten in Folge im Waikiki Shell in Honolulu, Hawaii, am 1. Juni.

Hendrix débute une nouvelle tournée américaine de 23 dates à la J.S. Dorton Arena de Raleigh (Caroline du Nord) - avec en soutien le nouveau groupe de Noel Redding, Fat Mattress. Elle s'achèvera après trois soirs au Waikiki Shell de Honolulu (Hawaii), le 1er juin de la même année.

### SATURDAY, MAY 3, 1969

Hendrix is arrested when he arrives at Toronto International Airport for a concert at the Maple Leaf Gardens. He is charged with possession of heroin and released on $10,000 bail. Rumors are rife that the Royal Canadian Mounted Police had been tipped off and were lying in wait for him.

Jimi Hendrix wird bei der Einreise in Kanada am Toronto International Airport verhaftet; er soll im Maple Leaf Gardens in Toronto auftreten. Er wird wegen Heroinbesitz angezeigt und gegen eine Kaution von 10.000 Dollar freigelassen. Das Gerücht geht um, dass ihn jemand an die Royal Canadian Mounted Police verraten hat, die ihm aufgelauert hat.

Hendrix est arrêté à son arrivée à l'aéroport international de Toronto, au Canada, où il doit participer à un concert au Maple Leaf Gardens. Il est accusé de détention d'héroïne et relâché après avoir versé une caution de 10 000 dollars. D'après la rumeur, la police montée canadienne avait été alertée et l'attendait.

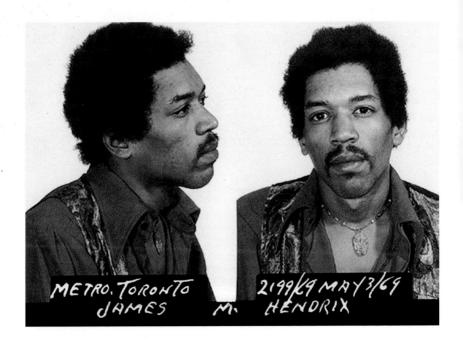

*"I want you to forget what happened yesterday and tomorrow and today. Tonight we're going to create a whole new world."*

*„Vergesst alles, was gestern und morgen und heute passiert ist. Heute erschaffen wir uns die Welt völlig neu."*

*« Je veux que vous oubliiez ce qui est arrivé hier, et demain, et aujourd'hui. Ce soir, on va créer un monde entièrement nouveau. »*

**JIMI HENDRIX, MAPLE LEAF GARDENS, TORONTO, MAY 3, 1969**

*"Jimi Hendrix has become another piece of apple pie in America."*

„Jimi Hendrix ist uns in Amerika mittlerweile so vertraut wie Apple Pie."

*« Jimi Hendrix fait maintenant partie du patrimoine de l'Amérique. »*

**VARIETY, 1969**

**THURSDAY, JUNE 19, 1969**
At a preliminary hearing in Toronto, Judge Robert Taylor rules that Hendrix will have to stand jury trial. The state prosecutor revealed that chemical analysis showed that powder found in a glass jar to be heroin, while a metal tube contained hash.

Bei einer Gerichtsverhandlung in Toronto befindet Richter Robert Taylor, dass Jimi Hendrix sich vor einem Geschworenengericht wird verantworten müssen. Der Staatsanwalt berichtet, dass sich das Pulver in einem Glasbehälter bei einer chemischen Analyse als Heroin erwiesen hat, in einem Metallröhrchen war Haschisch.

Au cours d'une audience préliminaire à Toronto, le juge Robert Taylor décide que Hendrix devra comparaître devant un jury populaire. Le procureur annonce que d'après les analyses chimiques, la poudre trouvée dans un bocal en verre est de l'héroïne et qu'un tube métallique contenait du haschisch.

### FRIDAY, JUNE 20, 1969

The first large-scale rock festival of the year—during
a ubiquitous period for festivals in general—Newport
69 gets underway at San Fernando Valley State College, at Devonshire Downs, California. The band is
paid $125,000—said to be the largest sum paid for a
single concert.

Das erste große Rockfestival des Jahres, Newport
69 – im Laufe des Sommers finden zahlreiche Open-
Air-Festivals statt – beginnt am San Fernando Valley
State College in Devonshire Downs, Kalifornien.
Die Gage der Band beläuft sich auf 125.000 Dollar –
angeblich die größte Summe, die bisher für
ein einzelnes Konzert gezahlt wurde.

Les festivals pullulent cet été-là. Le premier grand
rendez-vous pop de la saison, Newport 69, se tient sur
le campus du San Fernando Valley State College à
Devonshire Downs (Californie). Le groupe est payé
125 000 dollars, le plus gros cachet versé pour un
concert unique.

© Christie's

## SUNDAY, JUNE 29, 1969

The band plays its final concert together on the last day of the three-day "Denver Pop Festival" at the Mile High Stadium, Denver, Colorado. (Redding, after hearing Hendrix announce yesterday that former Army buddy Billy Cox is to be his new bassist, quits, to concentrate on Fat Mattress. Hendrix will spend the summer recording in New York with Cox and drummer Buddy Miles.)

Das Trio gibt sein letztes gemeinsames Konzert am Abschlusstag des dreitägigen „Denver Pop Festival" im Mile High Stadium, Denver, Colorado. Nachdem Noel am Vortag gehört hat, dass Jimi seinen ehemaligen Armee-Kameraden Billy Cox als neuen Bassisten ein-

setzen will, steigt er aus und konzentriert sich von nun an auf Fat Mattress. Jimi Hendrix verbringt den Sommer mit Billy Cox und Drummer Buddy Miles im Plattenstudio in New York.

Le groupe joue pour la dernière fois ensemble en clôture du « Denver Pop Festival », au Mile High Stadium de Denver (Colorado). (Redding, qui a entendu Hendrix annoncer la veille que son ancien camarade de régiment Billy Cox sera son nouveau bassiste, lâche le groupe pour se concentrer sur Fat Mattress. Hendrix passe l'été en studio à New York avec Cox et le batteur Buddy Miles.)

*"Hendrix is a brilliant technician and stylist, squeezing from his arsenal of guitars every shock of plugged-in power and psychedelic beauty. His fierce almost sadistic manipulation of the guitar's personality, is arrogantly featured in his act as he humiliates the instrument by raking it across the microphone stand, playing it disinterestedly behind his back, pushing up the volume till it whines out in pain and, finally, popping a string and discarding it altogether."*

*„Technik und Stil von Hendrix sind brillant, und er holt aus seinem Gitarrenarsenal jeden Elektroschock und jede psychedelische Schönheit heraus. Seine brutale, fast sadistische Manipulation der Gitarre und ihrer Persönlichkeit stellt er bei seinem Auftritt arrogant zur Schau: Er erniedrigt das Instrument, indem er es über den Mikrofonständer zieht, es lieblos hinter dem Rücken spielt und die Lautstärke so weit aufdreht, bis es vor Schmerz aufheult. Schließlich reißt eine Saite und er wirft es weg."*

*« Hendrix est un technicien et un styliste brillant, qui extirpe de son arsenal de guitares toute la puissance de la musique électrique et de la beauté psychédélique. Sur scène, il démontre avec arrogance la façon sauvage et presque sadique dont il manipule la personnalité de la guitare ; il l'humilie en la frottant au pied du micro, en la balançant avec mépris derrière son dos, en poussant son volume jusqu'à ce qu'elle gémisse de douleur et pour finir, en lui arrachant une corde. »*

**ED OCHS, BILLBOARD, 1969**

## MONDAY, AUGUST 18, 1969

Hendrix plays at the "Woodstock Music & Art Fair" in Bethel, New York, backed by the Gypsy Sons & Rainbows, drawn from musicians he has played with during the year. The set is highlighted by *The Star Spangled Banner*, a seminal performance captured on the "**Woodstock**" film and album. He is the highest-paid performer at the festival, earning $32,000 according to the promoters, although other sources have the figure as high as $125,000.

Jimi Hendrix tritt bei der „Woodstock Music & Art Fair" in Bethel, New York, auf. Begleitet wird er von Gypsy Sons & Rainbows, alles Musikern, mit denen er im Laufe des Jahres zusammen gespielt hat. Der Höhepunkt des Sets ist *The Star Spangled Banner*, eine herausragende Version, die im Film und auf dem Album **Woodstock** zu hören ist. Er erhält von allen teilnehmenden Musikern die höchste Gage, den Veranstaltern zufolge 32.000 Dollar, anderen Quellen zufolge sogar 125.000 Dollar.

Hendrix participe au « Woodstock Music & Art Fair » à Bethel, dans l'État de New York, avec le groupe The Gypsy Sons & Rainbows, composé de musiciens avec lesquels il a joué pendant l'année. Son set atteint des sommets avec sa version de *The Star Spangled Banner*, une performance mythique immortalisée dans l'album **Woodstock** et le film du même nom. Hendrix touche le cachet le plus élevé du festival (aux dires des organisateurs, Hendrix aurait perçu 32 000 dollars pour sa prestation, mais selon d'autres sources le vrai chiffre serait de 125 000 dollars).

"Sometimes when I come up here, people say 'he plays white rock for white people. What's he doing up here?' Well, I want to show them that music is universal – that there is not white rock or black rock. Some of these kids haven't got the $6 to go to Madison Square Garden – besides, I used to play up here myself at Small's over 135th and Seventh."

„Manchmal, wenn ich hier nach Harlem komme, dann sagen die Leute: ‚Der macht doch weißen Rock für Weiße. Was will der hier?' Ich will ihnen beweisen, dass es in der Musik keine Grenzen gibt – dass es keinen weißen Rock oder schwarzen Rock gibt. Einige der Kids haben keine sechs Dollar, um in den Madison Square Garden zu gehen – übrigens habe ich selbst hier früher oft gespielt, im Small's an der 135th und Seventh."

« Parfois, quand je viens ici, le gens disent : "Il joue du rock de blanc pour des Blancs. Qu'est-ce qu'il fout là ?" Eh bien, je veux leur montrer que la musique est universelle – qu'il n'y a pas de rock de Blancs et un rock de Noirs. Certains de ces gosses n'ont pas 6 dollars pour aller au Madison Square Garden – et en plus, moi aussi j'ai joué ici, chez Small's, sur les 135ᵉ et Septième avenues. »

**JIMI HENDRIX, UNITED BLOCK ASSOCIATION BENEFIT**

**FRIDAY, SEPTEMBER 5, 1969**

Hendrix gives a "Gypsy, Sun And Rainbow" benefit performance for the United Block Association on 139th St near Lenox Ave. in New York. (The week after the gig Hendrix will allegedly be kidnapped, although the circumstances are never made clear. Manager Michael Jeffery becomes the main suspect in the disappearance.)

Jimi Hendrix gibt ein Benefizkonzert „Gypsy, Sun And Rainbow" in New York auf der 139th Street in Harlem für die United Block Association. In der Woche nach dem Auftritt wird Hendrix unter nie geklärten Umständen angeblich gekidnappt. Der Hauptverdächtige bei seinem Verschwinden ist Manager Michael Jeffery.

Hendrix donne gratuitement un concert intitulé « Gypsy, Sun And Rainbow » pour la United Block Association, sur la 139ᵉ rue près de Lenox Avenue, à New York. (La semaine suivante, Hendrix aurait été victime d'un enlèvement dont les circonstances restent floues. Son manager Michael Jeffery est le principal suspect.)

**SUNDAY, NOVEMBER 2, 1969**
Hendrix begins work on his new **Band of Gypsys**
project with Buddy Miles and Billy Cox, recording at
the Record Plant with Alan Douglas producing.

Jimi Hendrix nimmt mit seiner neuen Formation
**Band of Gypsys** (Buddy Miles und Billy Cox) im Plattenstudio Record Plant die Arbeit auf, Alan Douglas
produziert.

Hendrix commence à travailler sur son nouveau
projet, **Band of Gypsys**, avec Buddy Miles et Billy
Cox ; ils enregistrent avec le producteur Alan Douglas
chez Record Plant.

© Hard Rock Cafe

**THURSDAY, NOVEMBER 27, 1969**
Hendrix, following three weeks of recording, celebrates his 27th birthday by attending the Rolling Stones' Madison Square Garden concert.

Nach drei Wochen im Aufnahmestudio feiert Jimi Hendrix seinen 27. Geburtstag als Zuschauer bei einem Konzert der Rolling Stones im Madison Square Garden.

Après trois semaines en studio, Hendrix fête ses 27 ans en assistant au concert des Rolling Stones, au Madison Square Garden.

**WEDNESDAY, DECEMBER 10, 1969**

After eight hours of deliberation, the jury at Toronto Court House finds Hendrix not guilty on charges of possession of heroin and marijuana. Hendrix testifies at his trial that he has experimented with drugs but has since "outgrown" the Jimi Hendrix experience. On his arrival in the city on Sunday for the trial, he was again arrested at customs for having drugs and spent the night in jail.

Nach achtstündiger Beratung sprechen die Geschworenen am Gericht in Toronto Jimi Hendrix vom Vorwurf des Heroin- und Marihuanabesitzes frei. Jimi Hendrix macht bei dem Verfahren die Aussage, er habe mit Drogen experimentiert, sei jetzt aber aus der Jimi Hendrix Experience „herausgewachsen".

Bei seinem Eintreffen in der Stadt am Sonntag wurde er allerdings am Zoll schon wieder verhaftet, weil er Drogen bei sich hatte, und verbrachte die Nacht im Gefängnis.

Après huit heures de délibéré, le jury du tribunal de Toronto juge Hendrix non coupable des délits de détention d'héroïne et de marijuana. Hendrix reconnaît sous serment avoir expérimenté les drogues mais affirme s'être depuis « lassé » de l'« expérience Jimi Hendrix ». À son arrivée en ville, le dimanche précédent, il a à nouveau été arrêté par les douaniers, qui ont trouvé de la drogue sur lui, et l'ont envoyé en prison pour la nuit.

### WEDNESDAY, DECEMBER 31, 1969

The Band of Gypsys debuts at the Fillmore East, New York, playing four sets over two days. The final two shows are recorded for the live album ***Band Of Gypsys***. As the New Year rolls in they begin playing their second set just after midnight with a rendition of *Auld Lang Syne.*

Die Band of Gypsys haben ihren ersten Auftritt im Fillmore East in New York, wo sie im Lauf von zwei Tagen vier Sets spielen. Die beiden letzten werden für das Live-Album ***Band Of Gypsys*** aufgezeichnet. Kurz nach Mitternacht, als das neue Jahr beginnt, starten sie ihren zweiten Set mit einer Coverversion von *Auld Lang Syne.*

Le Band of Gypsys fait ses débuts au Fillmore East, à New York, avec quatre concerts en deux jours. Les deux derniers sont enregistrés et deviendront l'album live ***Band Of Gypsys***. Le groupe commence son deuxième set juste après minuit, avec une version de *Auld Lang Syne.*

# 1970

*"It appears that Hendrix is finding where he should be at,
and he might well emerge as the greatest of the new blues guitarists."*

*„Es scheint, als wäre Hendrix gerade dabei herauszufinden,
wo es für ihn langgehen soll, und es ist gut möglich,
dass er als einer der größten neuen Blues-Gitarristen hervortreten wird.“*

*« Il semble que Hendrix commence à comprendre où est sa place,
et il pourrait bien devenir un des plus grands guitaristes de blues
de la nouvelle génération. »*

**CHRIS ALBERTSON, DOWNBEAT,
MARCH 5, 1970**

**WEDNESDAY, JANUARY 28, 1970**

With protests about United States involvement in the Vietnam War peaking, 19,000 fans attend the all-star "Winter Festival For Peace" benefit in aid of the Vietnam Moratorium Committee at Madison Square Garden. The Band of Gypsys set ends abruptly when Hendrix says, in response to Miles' statement—"I'm sorry we just can't get it together"—, "That's what happens when Earth fucks with space. Never forget that," and walks off stage in the middle of the second number, *Earth Blues*. The group will never perform again, with Cox returning to Nashville on Thursday.

Die Proteste gegen den Vietnamkrieg erreichen in den USA ihren Höhepunkt; 19.000 Fans kommen zum Star-Benefiz „Winter Festival For Peace" im Madison Square Garden zugunsten des Vietnam Moratorium Committees. Der Auftritt der Band of Gypsys endet abrupt, als Buddy Miles sagt: „Tut mir leid, wir kriegen's nicht auf die Reihe", und Jimi Hendrix erwidert: „So kommt's, wenn die Erde sich mit dem Weltall anlegt. Vergesst das nie." Daraufhin verlässt er inmitten des zweiten Stücks, *Earth Blues*, die Bühne. Die Gruppe wird nie wieder zusammen auftreten, Billy Cox kehrt am nächsten Tag nach Nashville zurück.

Alors que les manifestations contre l'entrée des États-Unis dans la guerre du Vietnam sont à leur apogée, 19 000 spectateurs assistent au concert de bienfaisance « Winter Festival For Peace » au profit du Vietnam Moratorium Committee, au Madison Square Garden. Le set du Band of Gypsys se termine brutalement quand Hendrix lâche, en réponse à une remarque de Miles (« Je suis désolé mais on ne va pas y arriver... ») : « C'est ce qui arrive quand la Terre fout la merde dans l'Univers. Ne l'oubliez jamais », et sort de scène au milieu du deuxième morceau, *Earth Blues*. Le groupe ne se produira plus jamais ensemble et Cox retourne à Nashville dès le lendemain.

**MONDAY, MARCH 23, 1970**

Having returned briefly to London, where he recorded with both Stephen Stills and Arthur Lee, Hendrix—back in New York—continues recording at the Record Plant, as the ***Band Of Gypsys*** album is released in the United States.

Jimi Hendrix war kurz in London zu Aufnahmen mit Stephen Stills und Arthur Lee und macht nun in New York mit den Einspielungen im Record Plant weiter. Gleichzeitig kommt das Album ***Band Of Gypsys*** in den USA auf den Markt.

Après un bref séjour à Londres, où il a enregistré avec Stephen Stills et Arthur Lee, Hendrix, de retour à New York, continue son travail chez Record Plant, alors que l'album ***Band Of Gypsys*** sort aux États-Unis.

*"The Experience is dead. That's like pages in an old diary."*

*„The Experience ist tot. Da ist nichts mehr als Seiten in einem alten Tagebuch."*

*« L'Experience est mort. C'est comme les pages jaunies d'un vieux journal intime. »*

**JIMI HENDRIX, MELODY MAKER, APRIL 15, 1970**

**SATURDAY, APRIL 25, 1970**

20,000 fans see the start of Hendrix's "The Cry Of Love" tour at the Great Western Forum in Inglewood, California.

20.000 Fans kommen im Great Western Forum in Inglewood, Kalifornien, zum Auftakt der Hendrix-Tournee „The Cry Of Love" zusammen.

20 000 fans assistent au lancement de la tournée « The Cry Of Love » au Great Western Forum d'Inglewood, en Californie.

*"At the end of the set Jimi broke into our national anthem and ordered us to stand up, which we did."*

*„Am Ende des Auftritts spielte Jimi unsere Nationalhymne und ließ uns aufstehen, was wir auch alle brav taten."*

*« À la fin du set, Jimi a joué les premières notes de notre hymne national et nous a demandé de nous lever, ce que nous avons fait. »*

**JUDY SIMS, DISC & MUSIC ECHO**

## SATURDAY, MAY 30, 1970

With the last three shows cancelled because of Hendrix's 'glandular problems', "The Cry Of Love" tour continues at the Community Theater in Berkeley, California.

Die „Cry Of Love"-Tour geht im Community Theater in Berkeley, Kalifornien, weiter. Die letzten drei Auftritte werden abgesagt, weil Jimi Hendrix „Drüsenprobleme" hat.

Les trois derniers concerts ont été annulés en raison de « problèmes glandulaires » dont souffrirait Hendrix, mais la tournée « The Cry Of Love » continue au Community Theater de Berkeley (Californie).

## MONDAY, JUNE 15, 1970

During a break in the tour, Hendrix goes into Electric Lady Studios in New York for the first time, jamming with Traffic's Steve Winwood and Chris Wood. On Tuesday, he will begin in earnest recording material for his next album.

Während einer kurzen Tourneepause geht Jimi Hendrix zum ersten Mal in die Electric Lady Studios in New York, wo er mit Steve Winwood und Chris Wood von Traffic jammt. Am nächsten Tag gehen die Aufnahmen für das nächste Album los.

Hendrix profite d'une pause dans la tournée pour essuyer les plâtres des studios new-yorkais Electric Lady par un bœuf avec Steve Winwood et Chris Wood, de Traffic. Le mardi, il commence les enregistrements pour son prochain album.

*"He sang adequately and generally unintelligibly, slammed the neck up and down the microphone stand, and went on his knees, to his back, picked with his teeth and indicated on a couple of occasions, that the guitar was not so much a guitar as an appendage of his lower body."*

*„Er sang durchschnittlich und im Allgemeinen unverständlich, knallte den Gitarrenhals an den Mikrofonständer, herauf und hinunter, ging auf die Knie, auf den Rücken, spielte mit den Zähnen und deutete mehrfach an, dass die Gitarre nicht so sehr eine Gitarre, sondern vielmehr eine Fortsetzung seines Unterleibs sei."*

*« Il a chanté convenablement, d'une manière inintelligible, a cogné le manche de sa guitare le long du pied de micro, est tombé à genoux, s'est roulé par terre, a joué avec les dents et montré à plusieurs reprises que la guitare n'était pas tant un instrument qu'un appendice de la partie basse de son corps. »*

**JOHN WASSERMAN, SAN FRANCISCO CHRONICLE**

## SUNDAY, JULY 26, 1970

Hendrix goes back to Seattle—for what will prove to be the last time—to play a hometown gig at Sicks Stadium. During the open-air concert—performed in pouring rain—Hendrix takes several verbal swipes at his experiences at Garfield High School.

Jimi Hendrix kehrt ein letztes Mal in seine Heimatstadt Seattle zurück, wo er im Sicks Stadium spielt. Das Open-Air-Konzert findet bei strömendem Regen statt, und Jimi Hendrix macht eine Reihe negativer Bemerkungen über seine Schulzeit an der Garfield High School.

Hendrix retourne à Seattle – pour la dernière fois – donner un concert au Sicks Stadium. Sous une pluie battante, Hendrix raconte quelques anecdotes sur sa scolarité houleuse au lycée Garfield.

## SATURDAY, AUGUST 1, 1970

Arriving in Hawaii on Tuesday, and beginning the filming of the Rainbow Bridge Vibratory-Color-Sound Experiment at Haleakala Crater in Maui on Thursday, Hendrix performs at the International Center Arena in Honolulu.

Jimi Hendrix ist am Dienstag auf Hawaii eingetroffen und hat am Donnerstag mit den Dreharbeiten zum Rainbow Bridge Vibratory-Color-Sound Experiment im Vulkankrater des Haleakala auf Maui begonnen. An diesem Tag tritt er in der International Center Arena in Honolulu auf.

Arrivé à Hawaii le mardi, il a commencé le tournage du « Rainbow Bridge Vibratory-Color-Sound Experiment » sur le cratère d'Haleakala, à Maui, le jeudi. Ce soir-là, il se produit à l'International Center Arena de Honolulu.

"It's going to be loud.
It will get louder. It will get loudest."

„Es wird laut werden. Es wird lauter.
Es wird so laut wie nie zuvor."

« Ça va faire du bruit.
De plus en plus de bruit. Le plus de bruit possible. »

**JIMI HENDRIX**

"It was a trip to Decibel City: a cacophony of electrical storms, coupled with a blizzard of frenzied artistry. It was loud and lethal for the senses, but the wizard of the whining guitar had warned his audience early in the program."

„Es war ein Trip in das Land der Dezibel: Eine Kakophonie elektrischer Hagelstürme, gepaart mit einem Ungewitter wahnsinniger Kunstfertigkeit. Es war laut und tödlich für die Ohren, doch der Großmeister der jaulenden Gitarre hatte das Publikum von Anfang an gewarnt."

« C'était un voyage à Décibel City : une cacophonie d'orages électriques mêlés à un tourbillon frénétique de talent. C'était assourdissant et fatal pour tous les sens, mais le magicien de la guitare gémissante avait averti son public dès le début de la soirée. »

**WAYNE HARADA, BILLBOARD, AUGUST 29, 1970**

### THURSDAY, AUGUST 27, 1970

After attending an opening party for Electric Lady Studios on Tuesday (it officially opened for business yesterday), Hendrix arrives at Heathrow Airport for his upcoming appearance at the Isle of Wight Festival. He will spend the next two days encamped at the Londonderry Hotel giving press interviews.

Nach der Teilnahme an der Eröffnungsparty der Electric Lady Studios am Dienstag (das Studio geht offiziell am nächsten Tag in Betrieb) trifft Jimi Hendrix am Flughafen London-Heathrow ein. Er verbringt die nächsten zwei Tage im Londonderry Hotel, wo er der Presse nonstop Interviews gibt, danach wird er beim Isle of Wight Festival spielen.

Après avoir assisté à la soirée d'inauguration des studios Electric Lady le mardi (ils ont officiellement ouvert leurs portes la veille), Hendrix arrive à l'aéroport londonien de Heathrow pour participer au festival de l'île de Wight. Il passe les deux jours suivants enfermé au Londonderry Hotel, où il donne des interviews.

### FRIDAY, AUGUST 28, 1970

In a day-long round of press interviews, Hendrix tells **Melody Maker**'s Roy Hollingworth: "It's all turned full circle. I'm back right now to where I started. I've given this era of music everything. I still sound the same, my music's the same, and I can't think of anything new to add to it in its present state."

Im Laufe der Gespräche mit der Presse, die den ganzen Tag dauern, erzählt Jimi Hendrix Roy Hollingworth vom **Melody Maker**: „Der Kreis hat sich geschlossen. Ich stehe jetzt wieder ganz am Anfang. Ich habe dieser Musikära alles gegeben. Ich klinge genau wie früher, meine Musik ist die gleiche geblieben, und mir fällt nichts Neues mehr ein, was ich ihr in ihrem derzeitigen Zustand noch geben könnte."

Au cours d'une journée d'entretiens marathon, Hendrix déclare à Roy Hollingworth, de **Melody Maker** : « La boucle est bouclée. Aujourd'hui, je suis de retour là où j'ai commencé. J'ai tout donné à cette génération musicale. J'ai toujours le même son, ma musique n'a pas changé, et je ne vois pas ce que je pourrais y ajouter de neuf dans l'état actuel des choses. »

### SUNDAY, AUGUST 30, 1970

In only his second United Kingdom appearance in three years, Hendrix comes on stage at 3:00 a.m. to play what will be his final performance in England, at the "Isle Of Wight Festival" at East Afton Farm in Godshill on the Isle of Wight. Assessing the event's overall success, Chief Constable of Hampshire, Douglas Osmond, says: "One of the good things has been the absence of violence. There is far less violence here than at a normal league football match," despite "the lunatic fringe," which he blamed for their attitude towards the police. Osmond says he had gone in casual clothes to sit among the people and listen to the music. "I found it very pleasant" he says.

Jimi Hendrix betritt die Bühne beim „Isle Of Wight Festival" auf der East Afton Farm in Godshill auf der Isle of Wight um drei Uhr morgens. Es ist erst sein zweiter Auftritt in Großbritannien innerhalb der letzten drei Jahre und wird sein letzter bleiben. Nach seiner Einschätzung zum Erfolg des Festivals befragt, sagt Douglas Osmond, der Polizeipräsident von Hampshire: „Einer der Pluspunkte ist die Abwesenheit von

Gewalt. Es gibt hier wesentlich weniger gewalttätige Vorfälle als bei einem normalen Fußballspiel", trotz „der radikalen Randgruppen", deren Verhältnis zur Polizei er kritisiert. Osmond berichtet, er sei in Freizeitkleidung zum Konzert gegangen, habe unter den Zuschauern gesessen und Musik gehört. „Es hat mir gut gefallen", sagt er.

Le deuxième concert britannique de Hendrix en trois ans, au festival de l'île de Wight, sera aussi son dernier concert en Angleterre. Hendrix entre en scène à trois heures du matin à l'East Afton Farm de Godshill. Le responsable des forces de l'ordre du Hampshire, Douglas Osmond, se félicite du succès de l'événement (« Une des bonnes choses, ç'a été l'absence de violence. Il y a eu bien moins de violence ici que pendant un match de football ordinaire ») malgré «une minorité de cinglés » qu'il accuse de s'être mal comporté avec la police. Osmond raconte comment il s'est mêlé à la foule, en civil, pour écouter la musique et affirme même avoir « trouvé ça très agréable ».

### SUNDAY, SEPTEMBER 6, 1970

Following bad experiences in Sweden (where Billy Cox took LSD before a concert), Denmark (when Hendrix left the stage after three songs with the words "I've been dead for a long time") and Germany (where the audience booed his late arrival), Hendrix makes what will prove to be his final concert appearance at the "Love And Peace Festival" on the Isle of Fehmarn in Germany.

Nach unerfreulichen Zwischenfällen in Schweden (wo Billy Cox vor einem Konzert LSD nimmt), Dänemark (wo Jimi Hendrix nach drei Songs die Bühne mit den Worten „Ich bin schon lange tot" verlässt) und Deutschland (wo er wegen verspätetem Erscheinen auf der Bühne ausgebuht wird) hat Jimi Hendrix seinen letzten Konzertauftritt beim „Love-and-Peace-Festival" am Leuchtturm Flügge auf der Insel Fehmarn.

Après de mauvaises expériences en Suède (où Billy Cox prend du LSD avant un concert), au Danemark (où Hendrix quitte la scène après trois chansons sur les mots : « Je suis mort depuis longtemps ») et en Allemagne (où le public hue son entrée en scène tardive), Hendrix donne ce qui sera son dernier concert au festival « Love And Peace » sur l'île de Fehmarn, en Allemagne.

## THURSDAY, SEPTEMBER 10, 1970

Having returned from Germany and booked into a £17-per-night room at the Cumberland Hotel, Hendrix attends a party for ex-Monkee Mike Nesmith at the Inn On The Park hotel.

Jimi Hendrix ist aus Deutschland zurückgekehrt, mietet sich in dem Billighotel Cumberland ein und nimmt an einer Party für den Ex-Monkee Mike Nesmith im Inn On The Park Hotel teil.

De retour d'Allemagne, Hendrix sort de sa chambre du Cumberland Hotel à 17 livres sterling la nuit pour assister à une fête organisée par l'ex-Monkey Mike Nesmith à l'hôtel Inn On The Park.

## WEDNESDAY, SEPTEMBER 16, 1970

Hendrix jams with Eric Burdon and War at Ronnie Scott's in London, before heading off to dinner on the Fulham Road, with a party which includes producer Alan Douglas and record company executive Danny Secunda.

Jimi Hendrix jammt mit Eric Burdon und War im Ronnie Scott's in London, danach nimmt er an einem Dinner in der Fulham Road teil. Bei der Party sind auch die Produzenten Alan Douglas und der Plattenlabelchef Danny Secunda dabei.

Hendrix donne un bœuf avec Eric Burdon et War au Ronnie Scott's, à Londres, avant d'aller dîner sur Fulham Road avec une bande d'amis, parmi lesquels le producteur Alan Douglas et le patron de maison de disques Danny Secunda.

*"He has more guitar skill in his little pinky than most of his blues-based contemporaries have in all of their phalanges combined."*

*„Er hat mehr Können in seinem kleinen Finger als die meisten seiner vom Blues kommenden Zeitgenossen in allen Gliedmaßen zusammen."*

*« Il a plus de talent à la guitare dans son seul petit doigt que la plupart des bluesmen contemporains dans toutes leurs phalanges. »*

**JAZZ & POP, SEPTEMBER 1970**

*"The story of life is quicker than the wink of an eye.
The story of love is hello, and goodbye, until we meet again."*

*„Die Geschichte des Lebens ist schneller vorbei ist als ein
Augenzwinkern. Die Geschichte der Liebe ist Hello und
Goodbye, bis wir uns wiedersehn."*

*« L'histoire de la vie passe plus vite qu'un clin d'œil. L'histoire
de l'amour, c'est bonjour, bonsoir, jusqu'à ce qu'on se retrouve. »*

**JIMI HENDRIX, SEPTEMBER 17, 1970**

## FRIDAY, SEPTEMBER 18, 1970

An ambulance is called to the basement flat of Hendrix's girlfriend, Monika Dannemann—Room 507 at the Samarkand Hotel at 22, Lansdowne Crescent, Notting Hill, London—where ambulancemen find his motionless body with vomit around his mouth. Dannemann, whom Hendrix met at a bar at Dusseldorf's Park Hotel in January of last year, has dialed the emergency 999 number, having been unable to wake him. He had apparently taken nine of her Vesperax sleeping pills. Hendrix is placed in the back of the ambulance and driven to St. Mary Abbot's Hospital in Kensington, where he is pronounced dead on arrival. The cause of death following an inquest next Monday, is given as "Inhalation of vomit, Barbiturate intoxication (quinal-barbitone). Insufficient evidence of circumstances, open verdict." The coroner, Gavin Thurston, will estimate that Hendrix—age 27—died at approximately 5:30 a.m. in his sleep. (Conspiracy theorists will continue to claim his death was not accidental, pointing to either suicide or even Danneman being complicit. In 1993, it will be announced that "Scotland Yard so far has been requested by the Crown Prosecution Service to conduct inquiries into the circumstances of the death of Jimi Hendrix." Nothing will come of it.)

Ein Notarztwagen wird zum Souterrain-Apartment von Jimi Hendrix' Freundin Monika Dannemann gerufen – Zimmer 507 im Samarkand Hotel in Lansdowne Crescent 22, Notting Hill, London. Die Sanitäter finden Jimi Hendrix bewegungslos mit Erbrochenem am Mund auf. Monika Dannemann, die ihn im Januar des Vorjahres an der Bar des Düsseldorfer Park Hotels kennengelernt hatte, hat die Notrufnummer 999 gewählt, nachdem sie ihn nicht wach bekommen konnte. Wie es scheint, hat er neun von ihren Vesperax-Schlaftabletten geschluckt. Jim Hendrix wird mit dem Krankenwagen abtransportiert und nach Eintreffen im St. Mary Abbot's Hospital in Kensington für tot erklärt. Nach der gerichtlichen Untersuchung wird als Todesursache am folgenden Montag angegeben: „Einatmen von Erbrochenem, Barbiturat-Vergiftung (Vesperax). Unzureichende Beweislage, abschließendes Urteil offen." Der Gerichtsmediziner Gavin Thurston erklärt, dass Jimi Hendrix im Alter von 27 Jahren um ca. 5 Uhr 30 im Schlaf gestorben ist. (Verschwörungstheoretiker behaupten weiterhin, sein Tod sei kein Unfall gewesen, sondern Selbstmord, manche Stimmen behaupten sogar, Monika Dannemann trage eine Mitschuld. 1993 wurde verlautbar: „Die britische Staatsanwaltschaft hat Scotland Yard aufgefordert, die Todesumstände von Jimi Hendrix zu untersuchen." Die Untersuchung war ergebnislos.)

Une ambulance est appelée chez la petite amie de Hendrix, Monika Dannemann – suite 507 du Samarkand Hotel, 22 Lansdowne Crescent, dans le quartier londonien de Notting Hill. Les ambulanciers y découvrent le corps inanimé de l'artiste, dont la bouche est barbouillée de vomi. Dannemann, que Hendrix a rencontrée au bar du Park Hotel de Dusseldorf en janvier de l'année précédente, a appelé les secours parce qu'elle ne parvenait pas à le réveiller. Il aurait pris neuf de ses somnifères. Hendrix est conduit à l'hôpital St. Mary Abbot de Kensington, où le médecin prononce immédiatement son décès. Le lundi, les enquêteurs annoncent la cause de sa mort : « Inhalation de vomi, intoxication aux barbituriques (quinalbarbitone). Preuves circonstancielles insuffisantes, conclusions ouvertes. » Le médecin légiste, Gavin Thurston, estime l'heure de la mort de Hendrix – âgé de 27 ans – à 5h30. (Les théoriciens du complot affirmeront que sa mort n'était pas accidentelle et qu'il s'agit d'un suicide, dont Danneman aurait même été complice. En 1993, Scotland Yard annonce qu'il lui a été demandé « par le bureau du Ministère public de la Couronne de mener une nouvelle enquête sur les circonstances de la mort de Jimi Hendrix ». Rien n'en sortira.)

"The death of 27-year-old U.S. rock star
Jimi Hendrix in London again spotlights the
destructive kicks fancied by the contemporary
music makers. The pursuit of exotic pleasure by
the new generation of pop stars may not be
different from the booze drinking of the old jazz
stars, but the tempo is faster."

„Der Tod des 27-jährigen amerikanischen
Rockstars Jimi Hendrix in London lenkt die
Aufmerksamkeit wieder einmal auf die
zerstörerischen Kicks, die von den
zeitgenössischen Musikern bevorzugt werden.
Die Jagd der neuen Generation von Popstars
nach exotischen Sinnenfreuden ist vielleicht
nichts anderes als die Trinkerei der alten Jazz-
Größen, aber das Tempo ist wesentlich höher."

« La mort à Londres, à seulement 27 ans, de la
rock star américaine Jimi Hendrix souligne une
fois encore les tendances destructrices auxquelles
cèdent les musiciens contemporains. La quête de
plaisirs exotiques dans laquelle se précipite la
nouvelle génération de pop stars ne diffère peut-
être pas tant que cela de la consommation
d'alcool des vieilles vedettes du jazz, mais l'issue
est plus rapide. »

**VARIETY, SEPTEMBER 23, 1970**

"The most important guitar player of any
generation: an absolute genius—and I don't use
that word lightly. A man completely in control of
every sound that emanated from his guitar."

„Der wichtigste Gitarrist nicht nur seiner, sondern
aller Generationen: Ein wahres Genie - und ich
benutze das Wort nicht häufig. Ein Mann, der
jeden Ton, der aus seiner Gitarre kam, völlig unter
Kontrolle hatte."

« Le plus grand guitariste de tous les temps :
un véritable génie - et je pèse mes mots.
Un homme qui maîtrisait à la perfection chaque
son qui sortait de son instrument. »

**EDDIE KRAMER, APRIL 2009**

*"When I die, I want people to play my music,
go wild and freak out and do anything they want to do."*

*„Wenn ich sterbe, dann sollen die Leute meine Musik spielen,
ausflippen und machen, was sie wollen."*

*« Quand je mourrai, je veux que les gens jouent ma musique, se défoulent,
pètent les plombs et fassent tout ce qui leur passe par la tête. »*

**JIMI HENDRIX**

*"Seattle-born rock superstar, whose grating, bluesy voice, screechy,
pulsating guitar solos and pelvis-pumping stage antics conveyed both a
turned-on, fetid sense of eroticism and, at best, a reverberated musical
equivalent of the urban black's anguished spirit."*

*„Der in Seattle geborene Rock-Superstar, dessen raspelige Blues-
Stimme, kreischende, pulsierende Gitarrensoli und beckenkreisendes
Bühnengebahren eine zugedröhnte, schwüle Art der Erotik vermittelten,
war im besten Fall das musikalische Wah-Wah-Äquivalent des
problemgeplagten Lebens der schwarzen Stadtbevölkerung."*

*« Avec sa voix crissante et bluesy, ses solos de guitare stridents et
palpitants et ses déhanchements publics, la superstar du rock originaire de
Seattle exprimait à la fois un érotisme exalté et nauséabond et, au mieux,
le reflet musical des angoisses de la population noire urbaine. »*

**TIME, SEPTEMBER 28, 1970**

### THURSDAY, OCTOBER 1, 1970
Following a funeral service at the Dunlap Baptist
Church, in Seattle, Washington (where his aunt played
organ during his childhood), Jimi Hendrix is buried at
Greenwood Memorial Park in nearby Renton. On his
gravestone, the inscription, "Forever In Our Hearts
James 'Jimi' Hendrix 1942-1970." Miles Davis, Johnny
Winter, Noel Redding and Mitch Mitchell attend the
service.

Nach einer Trauerfeier in der Dunlap Baptist
Church in Seattle, Washington (wo seine Tante in
seiner Kindheit Orgel spielte), wird Jimi Hendrix auf
dem Greenwood Memorial Park beigesetzt, der ca.
20 Fahrminuten außerhalb des Ortes liegt. Auf seinem
Grabstein steht: „Forever In Our Hearts James ‚Jimi'
Hendrix 1942-1970." Miles Davis, Johnny Winter, Noel
Redding und Mitch Mitchell nehmen an der Beerdi-
gung teil.

Après un service funéraire à l'église baptiste
Dunlap de Seattle (État de Washington), Jimi Hendrix
est inhumé au Greenwood Memorial Park, à vingt
minutes de la ville en voiture. Sur sa pierre tombale est
inscrit : « Pour toujours dans nos cœurs James "Jimi"
Hendrix 1942-1970. » Miles Davis, Johnny Winter, Noel
Redding et Mitch Mitchell assistent à la cérémonie.

# POSTSCRIPT

## POSTSKRIPTUM

## POST-SCRIPTUM

**WEDNESDAY, JANUARY 15, 1992**

Neil Young posthumously inducts the Jimi Hendrix Experience into the Rock and Roll Hall of Fame at the seventh annual dinner, held at New York's Waldorf-Astoria Hotel.

Neil Young fait entrer le Jimi Hendrix Experience au Rock and Roll Hall of Fame à titre posthume au cours du septième dîner annuel de l'organisation, à l'hôtel Waldorf-Astoria de New York.

Neil Young führt The Jimi Hendrix Experience beim siebten Jahresdinner im New Yorker Waldorf-Astoria Hotel posthum in die Rock and Roll Hall of Fame ein.

*"Jimi was a genius. He had a natural feel and did things his way— when you can do that and become accepted you're very different."*

*„Jimi war ein Genie. Er hatte von Natur aus das gewisse Feeling und machte alles auf seine unverwechselbare Art. Wenn man das hinbekommt und damit akzeptiert wird, dann ist man wirklich etwas ganz Besonderes."*

*« Jimi était un génie. Il avait un instinct naturel et faisait les choses à sa manière - quand on peut faire ça et être accepté, c'est qu'on est très différent. »*

**BILLY COX, 1971**

### FRIDAY, JULY 28, 1995

After a two-year legal battle, Al Hendrix finally wins control over all of his son's music in a settlement worth an estimated $70m. With the help of Microsoft co-founder Paul Allen—who is planning a Hendrix-inspired museum in Seattle—Hendrix senior had sued attorney Leo Branton Jr. for mismanaging his son's copyrights and master recordings. (Following Al's death in 2002, a new round of litigation will begin between his adopted daughter, Janie and Jimi's brother, Leon, a dispute over Al's will and Jimi's estate that will be resolved in Janie's favor in 2005.)

Nach einem zwei Jahre währenden Rechtsstreit werden Al Hendrix die Rechte an der gesamten Musik seines Sohnes zugesprochen, die auf einen Wert von 70 Mio. US-Dollar geschätzt wird. Unter Mithilfe des Microsoft-Mitbegründers Paul Allen – der ein von Jimi Hendrix inspiriertes Museum in Seattle bauen lassen will – hat Hendrix Senior den Anwalt Leo Branton Jr. wegen Missmanagement der Urheberrechte und Masterbänder seines Sohnes verklagt. Nach Al Hendrix' Tod 2002 gehen die Prozesse wieder los, diesmal zwischen seiner adoptierten Tochter Janie und Jimis Bruder Leon. Der Rechtsstreit um Al Hendrix' Testament und Jimis Nachlass wird 2005 zugunsten von Janie entschieden.

Après une bataille judiciaire de deux ans, Al Hendrix est jugé dépositaire de toute l'œuvre de son fils aux termes d'un accord estimé à quelque 70 millions de dollars. Avec l'aide du cofondateur de Microsoft Paul Allen – qui prévoit de créer un musée Hendrix à Seattle – Hendrix père avait attaqué l'avocat Leo Branton Jr. pour sa mauvaise gestion des droits d'auteur et des enregistrements originaux de son fils. (Après la mort d'Al, en 2002, de nouveaux contentieux éclateront entre sa fille adoptive Janie et le frère de Jimi, Leon, autour du testament d'Al et des biens de Jimi, litiges qui seront résolus en faveur de Janie en 2005.)

### TUESDAY, JANUARY 21, 1997

A statue of Hendrix is unveiled on the corner of Broadway and Pine in Seattle.

Une statue de Hendrix est dévoilée à l'angle de Broadway et de Pine, à Seattle.

An der Straßenecke Broadway und Pine in Seattle wird eine Plastik von Jimi Hendrix enthüllt.

**TUESDAY, APRIL 8, 1997**

*Are You Experienced*, *Axis: Bold As Love*, *Electric Ladyland* and *First Rays Of The New Rising Sun*, the first fruits of a worldwide licensing recent agreement between the Hendrix's family company, Experience Hendrix and MCA Records, announced at a press conference at Universal City's Hard Rock Café in January, are all released on heavy-gauge vinyl, with CD issue due in two weeks.

Die Alben *Are You Experienced*, *Axis: Bold As Love*, *Electric Ladyland* und *First Rays Of The New Rising Sun* kommen auf Vinyl neu heraus, die CD-Versionen zwei Wochen später. Diese Neuveröffentlichungen sind die ersten Früchte eines weltweiten Lizenzvertra-

ges zwischen der Hendrix-Familie, Experience Hendrix und MCA Records und wurden im Januar bei einer Pressekonferenz im Hard Rock Café in Universal City bekannt gegeben.

*Are You Experienced*, *Axis: Bold As Love*, *Electric Ladyland* et *First Rays Of The New Rising Sun*, premiers fruits d'un accord de commercialisation internationale conclu entre les héritiers de Hendrix et la maison de disques MCA Records, sont présentés à la presse au Hard Rock Café d'Universal City en janvier ; ils sortent tous en vinyle et les CD suivent deux semaines plus tard.

# 3

# ESSENTIAL RECORDINGS

## DIE WICHTIGSTEN ALBEN

## PRINCIPAUX ENREGISTREMENTS

### ARE YOU EXPERIENCED
**(1967)**

**1** Foxey Lady **2** Manic Depression
**3** Red House **4** Can You See Me
**5** Love Or Confusion **6** I Don't
Live Today **7** May This Be Love
**8** Fire **9** 3rd Stone From The Sun
**10** Remember **11** Are You
Experienced?

### AXIS BOLD AS LOVE
**(1967)**

**1** EXP **2** Up From The Skies
**3** Spanish Castle Magic **4** Wait
Until Tomorrow **5** Ain't No Telling
**6** Little Wing **7** If 6 Was 9 **8** You
Got Me Floatin' **9** Castles Made
Of Sand **10** She's So Fine **11** One
Rainy Wish **12** Little Miss Lover
**13** Bold As Love

### ELECTRIC LADYLAND
**(1968)**

**1** ... And The Gods Made Love
**2** Have You Ever Been (To Electric
Ladyland) **3** Crosstown Traffic
**4** Voodoo Chile **5** Little Miss
Strange **6** Long Hot Summer
Night **7** Come On (Part One)
**8** Gypsy Eyes **9** Burning Of The
Midnight Lamp

### BAND OF GYPSYS
**(1970)**

**1** Who Knows **2** Machine Gun
**3** Changes **4** Power To Love
**5** Message To Love **6** We Gotta
Live Together

### THE CRY OF LOVE
**(1971)**

**1** Freedom **2** Drifting **3** Ezy Rider
**4** Night Bird Flying **5** My Friend
**6** Straight Ahead **7** Astro Man
**8** Angel **9** In From The Storm
**10** Belly Button WIndow

### RAINBOW BRIDGE
**(1971)**

**1** Dolly Dagger **2** Earth Blues
**3** Pali Gap **4** Room Full Of Mirrors
**5** Star Spangled Banner **6** Look
Over Yonder **7** Hear My Train A
Comin **8** Hey Baby (New Rising
Sun)

### LIVE AT FILLMORE EAST
**(1999)**
**1** Stone Free **2** Power Of Soul
**3** Hear My Train A Comin'
**4** Izabella **5** Machine Gun
**6** Voodoo Child (Slight Return)
**7** We Gotta Live Together

### JIMI PLAYS MONTEREY
**(1986)**
**1** Killing Floor **2** Foxey Lady
**3** Like A Rolling Stone **4** Rock Me
Baby **5** Hey Joe **6** Can You See
Me **7** The Wind Cries Mary
**8** Purple Haze **9** Wild Thing

### LIVE AT WINTERLAND
**(1987)**
**1** Prologue **2** Fire **3** Manic
Depression **4** Sunshine Of Your
Love **5** Spanish Castle Magic
**6** Red House **7** Killing Floor
**8** Tax Free **9** Foxey Lady
**10** Hey Joe **11** Purple Haze
**12** Wild Thing **13** Epilogue

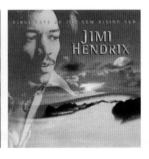

### RADIO ONE
**(1989)**
**1** Stone Free **2** Radio One Theme
**3** Day Tripper **4** Killing Floor
**5** Love Or Confusion **6** Drivin'
South **7** Catfish Blues **8** Wait Until
Tomorrow **9** Hear My Train A
Comin' **10** Hound Dog **11** Fire
**12** (I'm Your) Hoochie Coochie
Man **13** Purple Haze **14** Spanish
Castle Magic **15** Hey Joe
**16** Foxey Lady **17** Burning Of
The Midnight Lamp

### THE LAST EXPERIENCE
### CONCERT - HIS FINAL
### PERFORMANCE (1990)
**1** Little Ivey **2** Voodoo Child
(Slight Return) **3** Room Full Of
Mirrors **4** Fire **5** Purple Haze
**6** Wild Thing **7** Bleeding Heart
**8** The Sunshine Of Your Love
**9** Room Full Of Mirrors
(Extended Version) **10** Bleeding
Heart (Extended Version)
**11** Smashing Of The Amps
**12** C# Blues (People, People,
People)

### FIRST RAYS OF
### THE NEW RISING SUN (1997)
**1** Freedom **2** Izabella **3** Night Bird
Flying **4** Angel **5** Room Full Of
Mirrors **6** Dolly Dagger **7** Ezy
Ryder **8** Drifting **9** Beginnings
**10** Stepping Stone **11** My Friend
**12** Straight Ahead **13** Hey Baby
(New Rising Sun) **14** Earth Blues
**15** Astro Man **16** In From The
Storm **17** Belly Button Window

4

# AWARDS &
# CHART HISTORY

## AUSZEICHNUNGEN &
## CHARTPLATZIERUNGEN

## RÉCOMPENSES ET
## HISTORIQUE DES VENTES

## UNITED STATES CERTIFICATIONS
## UNITED STATES ALBUMS

*Rainbow Bridge* – Gold */ Hendrix In The West* – Gold */ Crash Landing* – Gold */ Axis: Bold As Love* – Platinum */ Smash Hits* – 2 Times Platinum / *The Ultimate Experience* – 3 Times Platinum */ The Cry Of Love* – Platinum */ Band Of Gypsies* – 2 Times Platinum */ Are You Experienced?* – 4 Times Platinum */ Electric Ladyland* – 2 Times Platinum */ Live At The BBC Session* – Gold */ Blues* – Platinum */ Live At Woodstock* – Gold */ Voodoo Child – The Jimi Hendrix Collection* – Gold */ Experience Hendrix* – 2 Times Platinum */ The Jimi Hendrix Experience* – Platinum

## UNITED KINGDOM CERTIFICATIONS
## UNITED KINGDOM ALBUMS

*Radio One* – Gold */ Cornerstones 1967-1970* – Gold */ The Ultimate Experience* – Gold */ Experience Jimi* – Silver */ Voodoo Child – The Collection* – Gold

## MISCELLANEOUS AWARDS

Performer of the Year 1968, Rolling Stone */* Rock and Roll Hall of Fame, 1992 */* Grammy Lifetime Achievement Award, 1992 */* Hollywood Walk of Fame, 1994 */* Blue Heritage Plaque, 1997 */* Purple Haze, Grammy Hall of Fame, 2000 */* The Greatest Guitarist of All Time, Rolling Stone, 2003 */* UK Hall of Fame, 2005 */* *Are You Experienced* inducted into United States National Recording Registry, 2006 */* Music City Walk of Fame, 2007

# US CHART HISTORY

## US CHART SINGLES

| Week of Entry | Highest Position | Wks | Title | Catalog Number |
|---|---|---|---|---|
| 94 (August 26, 1967) | 65 (October 14, 1967) | 8 | **Purple Haze** | Reprise 0597 |
| 80 (December 23, 1967) | 67 (January 13, 1968) | 4 | **Foxey Lady** | Reprise 0641 |
| 94 (March 16, 1968) | 82 (March 30, 1968) | 4 | **Up From The Skies** | Reprise 0665 |
| 66 (September 21, 1968) | 20 (October 19, 1968) | 9 | **All Along The Watchtower** | Reprise 0767 |
| 73 (November 30, 1968) | 52 (December 21, 1968) | 8 | **Crosstown Traffic** | Reprise 0792 |
| 99 (April 3, 1971) | 59 (May 8, 1971) | 8 | **Freedom** | Reprise 1000 |
| 89 (October 23, 1971) | 74 (November 27, 1971) | 7 | **Dolly Dagger** | Reprise 1044 |

## US CHART ALBUMS

| Week of Entry | Highest Position | Wks | Title | Catalog Number |
|---|---|---|---|---|
| 190 (August 26, 1967) | 5 (October 5, 1968) | 106 | **Are You Experienced** | Reprise 6261 |
| 194 (December 30, 1967) | 75 (February 17, 1968) | 12 | **Get That Feeling\*** | Capitol 2856 |
| 140 (February 10, 1968) | 3 (March 9, 1968) | 53 | **Axis: Bold As Love** | Reprise 6281 |
| 179 (October 19, 1968) | 1 (November 16, 1968) | 37 | **Electric Ladyland** | Reprise 6307 |
| 81 (August 2, 1969) | 6 (September 6, 1969) | 35 | **Smash Hits** | Reprise 2025 |
| 18 (May 2, 1970) | 5 (May 16, 1970) | 61 | **Band Of Gypsys** | Capitol STAO-472 |
| 53 (September 19, 1970) | 16 (October 17, 1970) | 20 | **Jimi Hendrix Experience\*\*** | |
| 18 (March 6, 1971) | 3 (March 27, 1971) | 39 | **The Cry Of Love** | Reprise 2034 |
| 132 (March 20, 1971) | 127 (April 3, 1971) | 4 | **Two Great Experiences/ Together** | Maple 6004 |
| 69 (October 9, 1971) | 15 (November 20, 1971) | 21 | **Rainbow Bridge** | Reprise 2040 |
| 43 (March 4, 1972) | 12 (March 25, 1972) | 19 | **In The West** | Reprise 2049 |
| 137 (September 2, 1972) | 82 (October 14, 1972) | 11 | **Rare Hendrix** | Trip 9500 |
| 171 (December 9, 1972) | 48 (February 10, 1973) | 18 | **War Heroes** | Reprise 2103 |
| 150 (July 14, 1973) | 89 (August 11, 1973) | 18 | **Soundtrack Recordings** | Reprise 6481 |
| 61 (March 22, 1975) | 5 (May 10, 1975) | 20 | **Crash Landing** | Reprise 2204 |
| 96 (November 29, 1975) | 43 (December 20, 1975) | 11 | **Midnight Lightning** | Reprise 2229 |
| 144 (August 12, 1978) | 114 (September 2, 1978) | 15 | **The Essential Jimi Hendrix** | Reprise 2RS 2245 |
| 180 (August 18, 1979) | 156 (September 8, 1979) | 7 | **The Essential Vol II** | Reprise HS 2293 |
| 181 (April 26, 1980) | 127 (May 24, 1980) | 7 | **Nine To The Universe** | Reprise 2299 |
| 140 (September 25, 1982) | 79 (October 16, 1982) | 8 | **The Jimi Hendrix Concerts** | Reprise 22306 |
| 182 (November 17, 1984) | 148 (December 8, 1984) | 5 | **Kiss The Sky** | Reprise 25119 |
| 197 (March 8, 1986) | 192 (March 15, 1986) | 3 | **Jimi Plays Monterey** | Reprise 25358 |
| 193 (December 3, 1988) | 119 (February 4, 1989) | 17 | **Radio One** | Rykodisc 0078 |
| 193 (January 5, 1991) | 174 (January 26, 1991) | 5 | **Lifelines – The Jimi Hendrix Story** | Reprise 26435 |
| 92 (May 15, 1993) | 72 (June 19, 1993) | 77 | **The Ultimate Experience** | MCA 10829 |
| 45 (May 14, 1994) | 45 (May 14, 1994) | 18 | **Blues** | MCA 11060 |
| 40 (August 20, 1994) | 37 (August 27, 1994) | 8 | **Jimi Hendrix – Woodstock** | MCA 11063 |
| 66 (April 29, 1995) | 66 (April 29, 1995) | 7 | **Voodoo Soup** | MCA 11236 |
| 49 (May 10, 1997) | 49 (May 10, 1997) | 11 | **First Rays Of The New Rising Sun** | Experience Hendrix 11599 |
| 51 (October 25, 1997) | 51 (October 25, 1997) | 6 | **South Saturn Delta** | Experience Hendrix 11684 |

| Week of Entry | Highest Position | Wks | Title | Catalog Number |
|---|---|---|---|---|
| 50 (June 20, 1998) | 50 (June 20, 1998) | 9 | **The BBC Sessions** | Experience Hendrix 11742 |
| 172 (November 21, 1998) | 133 (January 30, 1999) | 40 | **Experience Hendrix - The Best Of Jimi Hendrix** | Experience Hendrix MCAD-11671 |
| 65 (March 13, 1999) | 65 (March 13, 1999) | 4 | **Live At The Fillmore East** | Experience Hendrix MCAD2-11931 |
| 90 (July 24, 1999) | 90 (July 24, 1999) | 3 | **Live At Woodstock** | Experience Hendrix MCAD2-11987 |
| 78 (September 30, 2000) | 78 (September 30, 2000) | 3 | **The Jimi Hendrix Experience** | Experience Hendrix 112316 |
| 112 (May 26, 2001) | 112 (May 26, 2001) | 4 | **Voodoo Child - The Jimi Hendrix Collection** | Experience Hendrix 112603 |
| 200 (November 30, 2002) | 200 (November 30, 2002) | 1 | **Blue Wild Angel - Live At The Isle Of Wight** | Experience Hendrix 113086 |
| 191 (October 4, 2003) | 191 (October 4, 2003) | 1 | **Live At Berkeley** | Experience Hendrix 001102 |

# UK CHART HISTORY

## UK CHART SINGLES

| Week of Entry | Highest Position | Wks | Title | Catalog Number |
|---|---|---|---|---|
| 38 (December 31, 1966) | 6 (February 4, 1967) | 11 | **Hey Joe** | Polydor 56 139 |
| 39 (March 25, 1967) | 3 (May 6, 1967) | 14 | **Purple Haze** | Track 604 001 |
| 27 (May 13, 1967) | 6 (June 3, 1967) | 11 | **The Wind Cries Mary** | Track 604004 |
| 32 (September 2, 1967) | 18 (September 9, 1967) | 9 | **Burning Of The Midnight Lamp** | Track 604 007 |
| 48 (October 26, 1968) | 5 (November 30, 1968) | 11 | **All Along The Watchtower** | Track 604 025 |
| 37 (April 19, 1969) | 37 (April 19, 1969) | 3 | **Crosstown Traffic** | Track 604 029 |
| 15 (November 7, 1970) | 1 (November 21, 1970) | 13 | **Voodoo Chile** | Track 2095 001 |
| 50 (October 30, 1971) | 35 (November 13, 1971) | 5 | **Gypsy Eyes/Remember** | Track 2094 010 |
| 50 (February 12, 1972) | 35 (February 26, 1972) | 5 | **Johnny B. Goode** | Polydor 2001 277 |
| 61 (April 21, 1990) | 61 (April 21, 1990) | 3 | **Crosstown Traffic** | Polydor PO 71 |
| 52 (October 20, 1990) | 52 (October 20, 1990) | 3 | **All Along The Watchtower (EP)** | Polydor PO 100 |

## UK CHART ALBUMS

| Week of Entry | Highest Position | Wks | Title | Catalog Number |
|---|---|---|---|---|
| 22 (December 16, 1967) | 5 (January 13, 1968) | 16 | **Axis Bold As Love** | Track 613-003 |
| 21 (May 27, 1967) | 2 (June 10, 1967) | 33 | **Are You Experienced?** | |
| 40 (May 18, 1968) | 39 (May 25, 1968) | 2 | **Get That Feeling** | |
| 32 (April 27, 1968) | 4 (June 8, 1968) | 25 | **Smash Hits** | Track 613-004 |
| 23 (November 16, 1968) | 6 (December 7, 1968) | 12 | **Electric Ladyland** | Track 613-008/9 |
| 6 (July 4, 1970) | 6 (July 4, 1970) | 30 | **Band Of Gypsys** | Track 2406 002 |
| 2 (April 3, 1971) | 2 (April 3, 1971) | 14 | **The Cry Of Love** | Track 2408-101 |
| 15 (August 28, 1971) | 15 (August 28, 1971) | 6 | **Experience** | Ember NR 5057 |
| 17 (November 20, 1971) | 17 (November 20, 1971) | 2 | **Jimi Hendrix At The Isle Of Wight** | Track 2302 016 |
| 16 (December 4, 1971) | 16 (December 4, 1971) | 8 | **Rainbow Bridge** | Reprise K44159 |
| 45 (February 5, 1972) | 7 (February 19, 1972) | 14 | **Hendrix In The West** | Polydor 2302 018 |
| 40 (November 11, 1972) | 23 (November 18, 1972) | 3 | **War Heroes** | Polydor 2302 020 |
| 37 (July 21, 1973) | 37 (July 21, 1973) | 1 | **Jimi Hendrix Soundtrack** | Warner Bros. K64017 |
| 36 (August 30, 1975) | 35 (September 13, 1975) | 3 | **Crash Landing** | Polydor 2310 398 |
| 38 (March 29, 1975) | 35 (April 19, 1975) | 4 | **Jimi Hendrix** | Polydor 2343 080 |
| 46 (November 29, 1975) | 46 (November 29, 1975) | 1 | **Midnight Lightning** | Polydor 2310 415 |
| 59 (August 14, 1982) | 16 (August 21, 1982) | 11 | **The Jimi Hendrix Concerts** | CBS CBS 88592 |
| 86 (February 19, 1983) | 77 (February 26, 1983) | 4 | **The Singles** | Polydor PODV 6 |
| 30 (March 11, 1989) | 30 (March 11, 1989) | 6 | **Radio One** | Castle Collectors CCSLP 212 |
| 5 (November 3, 1990) | 5 (November 3, 1990) | 16 | **Cornerstones 1967-1970** | Polydor 8472311 |
| 30 (November 14, 1992) | 25 (November 21, 1992) | 26 | **The Ultimate Experience** | PolyGram TV 5172352 |

| Week of Entry | Highest Position | Wks | Title | Catalog Number |
|---|---|---|---|---|
| 10 (April 30, 1994) | 10 (April 30, 1994) | 3 | **Blues** | Polydor 5210372/ 5210374 |
| 32 (August 13, 1994) | 32 (August 13, 1994) | 3 | **Woodstock** | Polydor 5233842 |
| 47 (August 2, 1997) | 47 (August 2, 1997) | 1 | **Electric Ladyland** | MCA MCD 11600 |
| 37 (May 10, 1997) | 37 (May 10, 1997) | 2 | **First Rays Of The New Rising Sun** | MCA MCD 11599 |
| 21 (September 13, 1997) | 18 (September 27, 1997) | 15 | **Experience Hendrix - The Best Of Jimi Hendrix** | Telstar TV TTVCD 2930 |
| 42 (June 13, 1998) | 42 (June 13, 1998) | 2 | **The BBC Session** | MCA MCD 11742 |
| 10 (September 23, 2000) | 10 (September 23, 2000) | 7 | **Experience Hendrix - The Best Of Jimi Hendrix** | Universal TV/MCA 1123832 |
| 10 (July 20, 2002) | 10 (July 20, 2002) | 13 | **Voodoo Child - The Jimi Hendrix Collection** | Universal TV 1703222 |

# BIBLIOGRAPHY

**Black, Johnny:** *Jimi Hendrix The Ultimate Experience.* Carlton, 1999.
**Crampton, Luke & Dafydd Rees:** *Rock & Roll - Year By Year.* Dorling Kindersley, 2003.
**Cross, Charles R.:** *Room Full Of Mirrors - A Biography Of Jimi Hendrix.* Hyperion, 2005.
**Etchingham, Kathy:** *Through Gypsy Eyes.* Victor Gollancz, 1998.

**Lawrence, Sharon:** *Jimi Hendrix - The Man - The Magic - The Truth.* Harper Collins, 2005.
**Markel, Rita J.:** *Hendrix.* Lerner, 2001.
**Poole, Rebecca:** *Jimi Hendrix.* Lerner, 2006.
**Roby, Steven:** *Black Gold - The Lost Archives Of Jimi Hendrix.* Billboard Books, 2002.

# IMPRINT

© 2009 TASCHEN GmbH
Hohenzollernring 53, D-50 672 Köln
www.taschen.com

**Editor:** Luke Crampton & Dafydd Rees/
Original Media/www.original-media.net
**Picture Research:** Dafydd Rees & Wellesley Marsh
**Editorial Coordination:**
Florian Kobler and Mischa Gayring, Cologne
**Production Coordination:**
Nadia Najm and Horst Neuzner, Cologne
**Design:** Sense/Net, Andy Disl and Birgit Eichwede, Cologne
**German Translation:** Anke Burger, Berlin
**French Translation:** Alice Pétillot, Paris
**Multilingual Production:** www.arnaudbriand.com, Paris

Printed in China
ISBN 978-3-8365-1756-0

To stay informed about upcoming TASCHEN titles, please request our magazine at www.taschen.com/magazine or write to TASCHEN, Hohenzollernring 53, D-50 672 Cologne, Germany; contact@taschen.com; Fax: +49-221-254919. We will be happy to send you a free copy of our magazine, which is filled with information about all of our books.

**ACKNOWLEDGEMENTS**
Jessica Almonte, Mark Antman, Mitch Blank, Adam Chandler, Sara Fox, Tony Gale, Ralf Gartner, James Henke, Mike Kane, Elizabeth Kerr, Eddie Kramer, Elliott Landy, Rob Lifson, Matthew Lutts, Glen Marks, Joe Medina, Trish Murphy, Brian Pekny, Michelle Press, Michael Randolph, Elsa Ravazzalo, David Scripps, Jochen Sperber, Allan Tannenbaum, Kelly Wong

**COPYRIGHT**
The images in this book are copyright to the respective companies and photographers: Fiona Adams/Redferns/Getty Images: p. 54, Allposters.com: pp. 77, 78, 80, 86, 115b, 130, 158l / Associated Press: pp. 12, 38, 70t, 78, 106, 175 / Joel Axelrad/Michael Ochs Archives/Getty Images: pp. 137, 164, 165 / Bentley Archive/Popperfoto/Getty Images: p. 93 / Bettmann/ Corbis: p. 147 / Central Press/Getty Images: p. 160 / Mike Charity/Camera Press: p. 47 / Christie's: pp. 29t, 51r, 94b, 100, 109, 110, 123t, 136t / Roger Crump/Camera Press: p. 112 / Henry Diltz/Corbis: pp. 75, 115t, 140, 148 / Alain Dister/DALLE: 58 / Robert Edwards Auctions: p. 30 / Evening Standard/Getty Images: p. 124-125 / Express/Hulton Archive/Getty Images: p. 87 / Nat Farbman/Time Life Pictures/Getty Images: p. 24 / Bruce Fleming/Rex: pp. 43, 90, 91 / GAB Archive/Redferns/ Getty Images: pp. 70b, 83, 102, 116 / Jill Gibson/Michael Ochs Archives/Getty Images: pp. 19, 79 / Good Times-Photo: pp. 139, 167, 168 / Douglas Kent Hall/Zuma/Corbis: pp. 142, 143 / Hard Rock Cafe International (STP) Inc.: pp. 59b, 145r / Dezo Hoffmann/Rex: pp. 72, 94t, 95 / Ron Howard/Redferns/Getty Images: p. 128 / Hulton Archive/Getty Images: p. 29l / Hulton-Deutsch Collection/Corbis: p. 162 / Larry Hulst/Michael Ochs Archives/Getty Images: pp. 156-157 / Walter Iooss Jr./Getty Images: pp. 152-153, Endpapers / Mike Kane: p. 180 / King Collection/Retna UK: Cover, p. 6 / Eddie Kramer: pp. 132, 141, 146, 149 / Tony Kyriacou/Rex: p. 76 / Reg Lancaster/Hulton Archive/Getty Images: p. 44 / Elliott Landy: pp. 96, 104-105, 122, 170 / Elliott Landy/Corbis: pp. 64, 99 / London Features International: pp. 8, 11, 22, 32, 55, 69, 81, 92, 111, 114, Back Cover / Peter Macdiarmid/Getty Images: p. 68 / David Magnus/Rex: pp. 113, 176 / Stewart Mark/Camera Press: p. 123b / Fred W. McDarrah/Getty Images: p. 159 / Mirrorpix: pp. 89, 121 / Chris Morphet/Redferns/Getty Images: pp. 46, 50, 53 / Michael Ochs Archives/Corbis: pp. 172-173 / Michael Ochs Archives/ Getty Images: pp. 27l, 27r, 28, 31, 37, 85, 107, 108, 118, 119, 133, 136b, 161, 166, 174, 182 / J. Barry Peake/Rex: pp. 60, 66-67 / Jan Persson/Redferns/Getty Images: pp. 20, 84, 138, 150, 169 / Gilles Petard/Redferns/Getty Images: p. 36 / Pictorial Press: pp. 40, 48-49, 52, 56, 65, 73 / Robin Platzer/Twin Images/Time Life Pictures/Getty Images: p. 178 / PoPsie Photos: pp. 34-35 / Neal Preston/Corbis: p. 179 / David Redfern/Redferns/Getty Images: pp. 126, 131, 144-145, 163, / Rolls Press/Popperfoto/ Getty Images: p. 45 / Christian Rosel/DALLE APRF France: 16 / Herb Schmitz/Rex: p. 41 / Shepard Sherbell/Corbis SABA: p. 154 / Ray Stevenson/Retna Pictures: p. 71 / Ray Stevenson/ Rex: pp. 51l, 59t, 61, 62-63, 88, 101, / Allan Tannenbaum: pp. 2-3, 15, 117 / Topfoto/The Imageworks: pp. 98, 120, 129 / Courtesy by Universal Music Group: pp. 184-185 / Grey Villet/Time & Life Pictures/Getty Images: p. 25 / Val Wilmer/Redferns/ Getty Images: p. 42 / Zuma Press: pp. 103, 134, 135